American Elitism:
The Ideology of Oppression

For my son – may you finally have the peace that you deserved.
And may we all come to a better state of grace.

Table of Contents

Preface

While enjoying a drive home from a truly enchanting -albeit gentrified- community in northern New Mexico, I barely noticed as an old friend cued up a podcast hosted by a man who was only identified to me as a scientist. Still in my own reverie about how much the once quaint and special little town had changed, it occurred to me that a few ristras and new adobe walls could not restore the original mystique of the oldest capital city in the nation, no matter the amount of money spent to appease a few of its affluent residents. It then became clear to me that change, and change for the good, are two different things.

I became curious as I was drawn in to what at first sounded like a benign dialogue between two intellectuals. The book they were discussing was said to be one of the most controversial and provocative volumes of the past several years, which peaked my interest. I had heard little about the book, as I had been engulfed in my own career as a mental health professional and it had consumed all my time and attention. As the interview continued I became more and more interested. It appeared like the surviving co-author of the book, Charles Murray had written *The Bell Curve* with his colleague, Richard J. Herrnstein, who had passed away just prior to the book's publication.

Still, the controversy that the book generated seems to have lingered, as the date of the Murray interview was fairly recent. And it appeared that Murray had intentions of revisiting the text and reviving its contents after about twenty-five years. So I listened intently, curious as to what the book might offer and why it might have been so provocative.

At one point the author spoke of the harshness of his critics, even talking about biting commentary by those who had compared his work to *Mein Kampf,* which at the time seemed a little overboard to me. I had only the interview and the commentary that we were listening to in making my assessment. I had also heard a little bit about the controversy that it had created.

By now, the New Mexico sky was a blend of vivid pastel colors, as though some mythical artist had been inspired by Mother Nature herself to paint the skyline. These colorful sunsets, which are not so unusual in the Southwest, have inspired many an artist and this spiritual-like experience held me spellbound for several seconds. When I returned from my musing I realized that, though I had no prior interest in The Bell Curve, it was something more visceral that prompted me to think about the interview so much. I had been challenged to investigate further, ordering a copy that very evening upon my return home. Later in the week the more I read, the more I can now say that my concerns with what was between its covers caused me to become impelled by something deeper. I only hope to offer a small but meaningful contribution to the community of thought with my own offering.

   After the 2016 elections and the anger, chaos and confusion that ensued I felt the need to speak to a much needed cultural paradigm shift. And while this was not initially intended to be a discourse for or against anything, I also felt a sense of urgency to share some ideas about how people can reach a place of such indifference to the suffering of others. I believe that the underlying intentions to resurrect ideas in the Bell Curve are dark and divisive, and detrimental to our common humanity. This led me to a more pragmatic approach in attempting to shine a light on our own human darkness. My efforts also involved seeing it all through more of a psychological lens. Studying the complexities of behavior and endless human struggle have always intrigued me. And with all the emphasis on science and intelligence, one would have to wonder how all of our science and our best thinking have led us to this place. Readers are encouraged to use their own judgment and common sense in making their own determinations. It is my sincere belief that we are now at the turning point, or at the point of no return. I believe that America holds the greatest chance for hope and promise, and the greatest possibility for failure and disappointment.

Introduction

As we begin our commentary, the first thing that is most noticeable about the Bell Curve is its emphasis on cognitive ability and the intense focus on the intelligence of one group over another. While this data certainly has its uses, exactly **what** it is used for becomes an area of concern, as well as a major talking point. It is immediately obvious that the conclusions and remarks that are drawn from the mountain of statistics presented are an attempt to support an ideology that could easily be construed as divisive and oppressive. It isn't difficult to see that the social hierarchy that has been fabricated by some, using science as a weapon, has had damaging effects on the public's attitude, as well as on the policies and agendas of like-minded politicians and business leaders. This social stratification may have some validity and usefulness, however from a psychological perspective, we also understand that it has the ability to activate something deeper and darker in the human psyche -a sense of alienation from others. It is the "us and them" thinking that prevents unity, inside and out. What we don't talk about is the pervasive *self-alienation* from where all this originates. We find ourselves at a critical place, where we are separated from nature, separated from each other, and separated from our own nature.

And while we will be discussing intelligence and the mind, it is also imperative that we speak in terms of the human *psyche*. To clarify, when we speak of psyche, we are not only talking about the conscious mind, we are also speaking of its unconscious element, termed the *subconscious* in Freudian psychology. And we consider both of equal importance.

In the Afterword of the book, the authors assure us with their prediction that: "When the Sturm and Drang has subsided, nothing important in the Bell Curve will have been overturned." Let us suggest that first of all, the need to -some twenty-five years later- foment and revive the turmoil and controversy over this volume in itself, should give any critical thinker pause for thought. It is not the data and statistics that need to be overturned in the Bell Curve, but rather the pejorative interpretations and subjective remarks of the authors that beg to be examined. We're told that the truth doesn't need to be invented or resurrected, it stands on its own. If we cloak ourselves in it, it is said to have the potential to guide and protect us. In this volume, we can only speak our own truth.

We actually believe that a person is not required to be an ivy league graduate to contribute to society, and neither are one's test scores or income a true measure of their worth. It is also clear that those of lesser means will not have the advantage of an ivy league education. In fact, we would posit that there are qualities and characteristics in a human being that are just as important as Spearman's "g factor," which the authors themselves say is an arguable concept. Some researchers have even posited that it is not a sound and solid theory about general intelligence. Classical scholars have determined that the best standardized testing can only do a reasonably good job of measuring general intelligence. Other factors besides intelligence may very well determine not only political, social and economic outcomes, but may also shape all our personal actions and behavior. We can see this played out individually and collectively in all our relationships on a daily basis.

As a preface to further observations we must also determine what success means to us on a personal level, since success is so closely associated to intelligence in the Bell Curve. Aside from obvious monetary and materialistic gain, status and power, other more practical definitions of success might be considered. An example is found in a more humanistic description of the term by the ever insightful, Ralph Waldo Emerson: *"To laugh often; to win the admiration of intelligent people and the affection of children; to earn the respect of honest critics and endure the betrayal of false friends; to apprehend beauty; to find the best in others; to leave this world a bit better whether by a healthy child, a garden patch or a redeemed social condition; to know that even one life has breathed easier because you have lived -that is said to have succeeded."* So intelligence and success **can** be viewed in a different light. In my personal and professional observations, it is interesting to note that intelligence alone does not always equate to what might be more commonly considered as a loving, caring, thoughtful human being.

Also observed within my own experiences were some of the qualities and characteristics that some people of high intelligence do not always display, e.g. sensitivity, compassion, empathy, and common sense. It is possible for people to be smart, but not reasonable. It is also possible for people to be considered as intelligent, but have little common sense. Specializing in a particular field, intellectualism and pedantry also come with a cost.

We are all the progeny of our past, whether we fully understand the deeper ramifications or not. We are all the products of our culture, our life experiences, our environment and how we were parented. Psychology and the social sciences teach us that vanity, arrogance, callousness and dispassion are rooted in that past and there is no better time than now for honesty, self-scrutiny and real change. While we have taken a big step forward technologically, psychologically we've taken two steps back.

We understand that human intelligence is important in all areas of our lives, however intellectualism seems to ignore and undervalue the vital importance of spirit and soul, and scientific rationalism would even question their existence. We are also aware of the fact that, while there is a great interest in those topics, there is actually a dearth of empirical research and data in this area.

We consider the human psyche in all of its manifestations as the last frontier. Focusing on only the material aspects of our lives denies the inexplicable phenomena that people experience every day. While the mind/brain controversy was never fully settled, there are some things that we can deduce. This thing that we call *consciousness*, directly related to intelligence, cannot fully be defined or explained any more than the *unconscious*. We also know that the use of the word *mind* has certain connotations that infer that the brain itself is the primary source of all thoughts, fantasies and emotions, although these extraordinary assertions have never been proven. This also infers that all of our feelings and experiences are merely the side effects of neurons and neurochemical activity, nothing more than byproducts of the brain.

In speaking to the ongoing mind/matter debate U.C.L.A. Professor of Psychiatry, Jeffrey M. Schwartz challenges the long held scientific position that the mind is an illusion and only a byproduct of the brain. This type of thinking creates not only the denial of a deeper psychic reality, it then sees the answers to all of our problems as being more materialistic in nature. This then leads to trying to find all the answers outside of ourselves. Even now, it is a commonly held belief among scientists and the highly educated, that the mind and the brain are synonymous, and that so-called mental illnesses are in reality merely brain disorders.

This materialistic mindset has many consequences. For example, empirical psychology taught us some time ago that there are essentially three types of the clinical disorder known as *depression*: environmental or situational depression, biological or chemical depression, and intrapsychic depression, the latter caused by an inner conflict that is not explained away by our biochemistry or what's going on at home. The point here is that while biological depression may actually account for only a small percentage of diagnosed depression, all three forms are generally considered as medical disorders, and all are treated in the same manner, with psychotropic medications. These chemical solutions all come with side effects that can become as harmful as the condition itself. And until recently, the value of talk therapy was ignored and minimized by many medical professionals. Even talk therapy itself may become harmful or less effective in the hands of those therapists who have limited experience, a personal agenda, or who just don't know themselves. "Physician heal thyself."

So when we begin to talk about cognitive ability, intelligence or mental health these things are not easily understood or defined by our limited tools of measurement. Along those lines, Dr. Schwartz further elaborates on mind/matter and the advent of scientific materialism, beginning with his thoughts about Sir Isaac Newton, a great thinker in his own right. Dr. Schwartz states that Newton essentially "eliminated the divine from the ongoing workings of the universe" while not personally believing in pure materialism himself. It has also been suggested that Newton's intense studies and passion for alchemy were in fact more of a spiritual endeavor than a scientific one. It is also important to note that Einstein, Newton, Jung and others all took an avid interest in the study of alchemy.

Schwartz also identified a dualist position in the thinking of the famous 17th century philosopher, Rene Descartes who was the first modern scientific thinker to seriously wrestle with the "strangeness of the mind." Simply summarized, Descartes' problematic view was that the mind and the body were thought of in mechanistic terms, in other words, the mind was thought of as a machine, which was subject to deterministic rules. The human body itself was considered an automaton. Schwartz goes on to declare that three and a half centuries later, Descartes' ideas still endure.

"If there is a single fundamental underpinning in the intellectual tradition of Western thought, it is arguably that there exists an unbridgeable divide between the realm of the material (which is definitely real) and the realm of the immaterial (which, according to the conventions of science, is likely illusory)." And the views and opinions of some our leading scientists and researchers have obviously been shaped and influenced by the great thinkers of the past. In a conclusive statement Schwartz remarks, "Materialism, it seems fair to say, has neuroscience in a choke-hold and has had it there since the nineteenth century." (*The Mind and the Brain*, 2002)

It is also clear that, in the scientific community, many other modern thinkers have weighed in on the limits of the Cartesian/Newtonian model of science, although its contributions are well respected. The current situation in this country and in this world is critical and we can only wonder how all our best thinking and decision-making skills led us to this point. In 1952 the insightful analyst, author and teacher, C.G. Jung aptly proclaimed that, "Not nature, but the genius of mankind has knotted the hangman's noose with which it can execute itself at any moment." Is this just the negative thinking of the past...or is it our modern reality?

As we look a little closer at our thinking processes, another thing we notice is that people are not always guided by their knowledge base and logical, rational thinking. Some studies indicate that our actions are preceded by our thoughts. But when looking at Post Traumatic Stress, following a traumatic experience, a state of shock often curtails thought processes and survivors are left with a sense of dread and utter disbelief (disassociation). Following a variety of PTSD studies which began with train crashes, and then studies of war survivors, it is commonly understood that the shock one experiences after a traumatic event is a mechanism by which the brain "protects" the victim from the immediate horror of the experience. In this state, thinking appears to be an activity that occurs after an emotional response, or the total lack of a response. In these cases, thinking becomes a secondary activity.

And those traumatic experiences are never completely forgotten. PTSD has more recently been recognized as a serious and legitimate mental health disorder affecting not only the survivors of war. Those same symptoms are found in survivors of severe physical and sexual abuse, and other traumatic events. While a variety of studies on this issue are available to the public, the Veteran's Administration itself has done extensive research on the topic, which is also available for review. We can only hope that ongoing studies will continue to change the outdated attitudes of the public and of our current policymakers. In essence, what these studies seem to suggest is that we are not always thinking creatures that feel, but rather feeling creatures that think.

Mentioned earlier, the psychology of the analyst, C.G. Jung has been at the forefront of understanding the human psyche at its deepest level, even though his work may be considered as unconventional and out of the mainstream. Pioneers in thought have always paid a price, as Jung's mentor and colleague Freud discovered before him. Often overlooked, underestimated and even demeaned, Jung's diligent efforts in understanding the unconscious psyche have endured. In the scientific research of human activity and behavior no other studies have seemed to provide us with an adequate explanation of the never-ending violence, unhealthy behavior and man's inhumanity to man.

Still, the advocates of scientific materialism remain doubtful and suspicious, even though manifestations of the unconscious continue to appear all around them on a regular basis. And scientific reductionism, along with causality, are not applicable when we attempt to examine the unconscious so their skepticism is relative and understandable. However, the scientists of their day also firmly believed that the world was flat and that the sun revolved around the earth, until science was forced into a new direction. What we once considered as our universe is now thought of as a *multiverse*. From Karl Popper to Ilya Prigogine we are now learning that our deterministic world view is fading and that new laws of nature are emerging in what Prigogine has described as "the end of certainty."

What is also observable is that aside from some strides in medicine and technology, science has recently made few groundbreaking accomplishments to speak of. There are also modern scientists and thinkers who believe that major scientific breakthroughs remain at a standstill and that science itself may have run its course so to speak. In fact, we opine that it is a sort of scientific arrogance that causes some scientists to believe that they have all the answers and that science and technology can solve all our problems, e.g. *The Theory of Everything* (T.O.E. as it is sometimes called). It is believed that, among other things, this theory might explain the beginning of the world as well as its ending, and even explain away God. And some have adamantly stated that they actually don't care to have their long-held and cherished beliefs obliterated by a researcher in a laboratory. Throughout this discourse we will continue to allude to *ego inflation*, and what we believe to be the pandemic of the modern world.

The great American thinker, Henry Ford once declared that, "Thinking is the hardest work there is, that's why so few people engage in it." However, even his high IQ and his creative mind did not prevent him from being a rabid anti-Semite, and his venomous hate for Jewish people was demonstrated for all to see, so intelligence doesn't seem to be a preventative for hate and animosity. When we speak about the psyche, the element that may be the impetus for much of our behavior could very well be the thing that we ignore and avoid the most, the *unconscious* element of the psyche.

In the study of *etymology*, we learn that the origins and development of words is appropriate for studies in psychology due to the often unconscious origins of the words themselves. When we look at the word *psyche* we discover that it comes from the Greeks and that its original meaning was "soul" or "spirit," so that the meaning of psychiatry for instance, was more about a study of the spirit or the soul; a far cry from today's interpretation of medicating the brain.

When we speak of intelligence and thinking, we are speaking about things that are far more complex than they appear to be. In accordance to the thinking of the pioneers of a deeper psychological understanding, i.e. Freud and Jung, the human psyche is composed of not only consciousness and our conscious thinking processes, but also the unconscious, which is believed to be a two-tiered structure comprised of the personal unconscious, and what has been termed the collective unconscious. The former has been shown to carry the past experiences, memories etc. of our personal lives and it seems more familiar to us. The latter is said to hold all the past experiences of the entire history of humankind. This may also be a place where psychology and the "pure" sciences part their ways.

It is very difficult to fathom the wide-ranging importance of these concepts, and for many, even more difficult to accept. As the scientific foundations of the Cartesian/Newtonian paradigm are coming more and more into question, this can be very unsettling to those who have so much invested in their subsequent discoveries and accomplishments. When we actually notice that we are not always in control of our thoughts and emotions, or that unaccountable images and flights of fantasy can enter into our minds without our desire and without our summoning, then we can begin to see the complexity of understanding the human psyche and thought, of which intelligence is just one facet. It's also interesting to consider that some important scientific discoveries began with an intuitive hunch or a dream. While full and detailed definitions of all these ideas are not within the purview of this volume, there is a considerable amount of information that is available on these subjects.

We are also aware that many of these scientific theories are just that - theory. As good scientists know, they themselves can only postulate and present theories, they cannot assert absolutes or fact. And particularly (post-Kantian) we understand that we can all only see things through our subjective lens. In other words, truth itself may be subjective. In fact, it has been posited that all phenomena and everything we observe in the spatio-temporal world is subjective, relative, protean and subject to change. When others profess to have the truth, or they attempt to define what it is for us, we should all hesitate and ask ourselves just whose truth it is. We propose that any descriptions or definitions about the mind and thinking are only partial explanations if they do not include the unconscious element of the psyche, and that consciousness and the unconscious need each other. Just as in the balancing act of nature itself, water seeks its own level. And as far as the elusive concept of truth is concerned, we finish our thoughts here with an ancient Chinese aphorism that it might do well to contemplate: "The greatest curse of the gods is to survive your own truth."

Leading up to our observations of the Bell Curve it is also important to note that manifestations of the unconscious psyche appear in various forms and images, e.g. dreams, visions, imagination, and even in fairy tales and ancient lore. And when attentive to these images the underlying symbolism appears to convey a personal message to those who are open to their meaning, and these are essentially metaphors for our lives. It also seems clear that these inner connections have the ability to take us out of our limited egocentric world, enabling us to live our lives with more depth and meaning.

So, to put so much emphasis on thinking and cognitive ability, while of obvious importance, is a fragmentary existence. Some psychologists would say that we have even sacrificed our feelings at the opposite end of the thinking spectrum. Psychologist and author, Dr. James Hollis has appropriately commented: "The mystery of which we are a fragmentary part is not only far beyond our capacity to engineer, but beyond even our power to comprehend." In what has been considered as a primarily extroverted, thinking society there is a strong tendency to ignore what is immanent in all humans, and to avoid our feelings. And why do we stress feelings here? Because our feelings are what make us human! In the words of Einstein's illustrious colleague and theoretical physicist, David Bohm, "The true state of affairs in the material world is wholeness. If we are fragmented, we must blame it on ourselves."

"Men will cease to commit atrocities when they cease to believe in absurdities."   Voltaire

Observations and Commentary

We begin our review with one small segment of the text (pp. 110-112) where focusing on I.Q. the authors make the case for the tendency to mate by cognitive ability. While there are definitely studies that indicate that heterosexual couples who share similar values, beliefs, etc. are more likely to maintain long-term relationships, intelligence is not the only measure in the mating process. In fact, in the world of counseling and therapy we've learned that other factors play a vital role in human interactions and in relationships. We believe that there is no more fertile ground for inner child issues and how we may have been parented than marriage and intimate relationships. Empirical psychology and clinical observation have shown time and time again that as long as parental complexes remain active in an individual, then he or she will consistently choose partners much like his or her parents, or compensate by choosing someone who is the opposite of their parents. *Complexes* can also be involved and they can be thought of here as latent clusters of negative energy that remain in the psyche and can be activated by certain triggers. Commonly seen in clinical settings, they are also observed in our daily lives and can be shaped around a variety of major issues: money, power, sex, marriage, family, etc.

While this all involves some use of intelligence, at the same time, we know that there is more often something deeper involved that works alongside our intelligence. When we add an understanding of the theory of *psychological projections* then we have more of a complete picture. It is common knowledge that projection is a natural event that occurs in all people. Basically, projections are a quality or characteristic within us that we perceive as outside of ourselves and then we project outwardly onto some other individual, group or organization. Projections can also be positive or negative. This is usually an unconscious or partially conscious process, so when these images are brought into the light and we are made aware of them, they appear to lose their power over us and are no longer considered as projection.

So it may be beneficial for us to become more aware of what's going on inside us so that we might project less onto others, which can become harmful and even dangerous (e.g. stalking). Relationships are not the only place where projections occur, and they happen on an individual and a collective basis as well. In his studies of more primitive societies, the anthropologist, Lucien Levy Bruhl made an important -albeit largely ignored- discovery. He realized that members in primitive tribes that he studied would actually go into a trance-like state when their unconscious was activated en masse. He named this collective state of mind *unconscious mutual identification.* This behavior can be seen in what we call mob mentality today.

The acceptable and even common practice of lynching in the South led to the murders of four thousand or more blacks, seemingly for no other reason than the color of their skin. The troubling behavior of the otherwise "normal" people involved in these violent crimes has not really changed. This is evidenced by the overt hate speech across the country, which is sometimes sanctioned by our own leaders. A more striking example is found in the 2014 lynching of a 17-year-old black boy (Lennon Lacy) in North Carolina. This is usually accompanied by a way of thinking that includes a callous sense of superiority, and the projection of one's own unchecked darkness onto a perceived enemy, usually someone who is different or somehow unacceptable.

So while our own conscious egos would have us believe that surely we choose partners consciously and with our intellects, this is only partially true. Some psychologists aver that most of our more serious relationships in particular, begin in projection. More often, we later discover that all that glitters is not gold. A common complaint with couples in marital counseling is that one of the partners will claim not to know their partner, "… after all these years." While this may be a valid complaint, it is difficult for a person to fully know the unknown side of anyone else, which makes for good ratings and TV drama, but doesn't deal with the deeper psychic reality. As mentioned, people with similar interests do tend to couple with those who are like-minded, but more extensive studies need to be conducted in order to establish causality and whether or not they actually marry "within their own ranks" solely due to intelligence.

The constant inference throughout this part of the text is that the cognitive elites are becoming more segregated, and yet these groups have always had a tendency to maintain their distance from those who are perceived as different or "less than." It seems clear that there are no mandates for this separation so this seems more like a matter of choice. The research that might be more revealing would be long term studies about how many of these cognitive elites remain with the same partner and how many of those marriages are still healthy and intact.

Some marriages stay together for the sake of the children, to maintain appearances, or maybe due to the potential loss of status or finances. And others have admitted to being fearful or intimidated about going out into the world, starting over again and possibly experiencing yet another failed relationship. Cognitive elitists don't seem to have the market on healthy, loving, lasting relationships, no matter how intelligent they seem to be. Loving, enduring relationships are not understood by simply testing for IQ, which seems to ignore the whole human being.

This also seems to promote a separatist attitude and advocates for a form of selective bonding, creating a wider chasm between groups and classes. If the initial exchange between a prospective couple begins with conversations over finances and IQ scores, some might find good reason to remain single. While some marriages do exist due to financial reasons, these relationships can seem more like business arrangements. However, even relationships that rely on dependency can thrive and serve a purpose for the involved parties, at least until a crisis or a simple twist of fate occurs. Selective mating ideas might also bring to mind the kind of thinking that facilitated inbreeding and the ill-conceived notion of eugenics.

Poverty

Following the progression of the narrative, Herrnstein and Murray then turn their attention onto issues surrounding poverty, as it relates to whites and their cognitive ability. The authors have stated that prior to 1960, and for three decades, the percentage of those below the poverty line actually decreased, however there is also an abundance of information that indicates that this all began to change during the Reagan administration. It's clear now that Reagan's austere policies and the "trickle down" theory actually trickled up, while the assault on programs that attempted to lift people out of poverty began. Unfortunately, the authors may have missed all the data that pointed to a dramatic increase in homelessness, increases in unemployment, decreases in workers' wages and benefits, along with other harmful practices that have only increased over the past several decades. From a human perspective one can only guess at why some would want to keep people in the throes of poverty and deprivation. And we have recently learned of researchers and statisticians who manipulate the data for their own self-serving purposes, and for a much larger sociopolitical agenda, rendering their findings at least suspect.

And of course there will always be those who choose to believe that poverty is a natural or even necessary thing. In this section of the book (p. 138) the poverty of children in the U.S. is blamed on mothers of low intelligence. We don't recall anyone ever asking just how many of those impoverished mothers actually chose to be poor. The view of the authors is clearly stated, "The way to avoid poverty in the United States is to be born into an advantaged family," as if people had a choice as to what family they were born into in the first place. This statement appears to have some validity, however the choice of the term "avoid" would suggest that people could decide their family of origin -or their skin color for that matter. And this would help them avoid prejudicial treatment later, if it were possible. To have that choice would be a nice option because there probably aren't many people who would choose to be disadvantaged. However, there are actually a few people left in the world whose ethics would not allow them to compromise themselves for wealth and comfort, even if given a choice.

Most people are aware of the fact that poverty serves a purpose. In fact, there have been several publications outlining just how big business and corporations actually cash in on the poverty itself (e.g. *Merchants of Misery* by Michael Hudson). And while there may be those people who are less motivated and less industrious than others, to lump them all together and then set upon them with punitive laws and policies, is to blame and judge the many for the actions of a few. It's like blaming all the wealthy for the callous actions of a few people, who are just plain greedy.

In the wealthiest country in the world, some economists have estimated that one out of every four children lives in poverty. In a country professing justice, equality and opportunity, how can such a thing be so? Gandhi once commented that the greatest crime perpetrated on people was poverty. In America today, polls have shown over and over that a vast majority of people believe in God and that they subscribe to the Christian principles of love and charity, however their actions and behavior might suggest something entirely different. To shine a light on how Christ himself felt about the issues of poverty and morality we simply turn to the words of the man of love and peace, and the very scriptures that so many good Americans profess to believe in:

I was hungry and you gave me food; thirsty and you gave me drink; I was a stranger and you made me welcome; naked and you clothed me. I tell you solemnly, in so far as you did this to one of the least of these brothers of mine, you did it to me Matt. 25: 35-36. We find in these lines no mention of one's level of intelligence, skin color or cognitive ability.

It has been estimated that one out of every four children in the richest country in the world lives in poverty, and yet this vital issue is never even mentioned in today's politics, as if it didn't even exist. At the heart of the matter are the core principles of the tradition we've inherited (e.g. "agape") which appear to be in accord with the man of peace and love, so highly loved and revered by his followers.

And yet the sordid actions and behavior of these followers (e.g. today's hateful and self-serving politicians) indicate the opposite of what is presented to the public. And the word that generally describes this moral dilemma is "hypocrisy." "For what does it profit a man to gain the world and lose his soul."

Blaming the Victim

The title of this portion of our commentary is self-explanatory, and it seems like American politicians and other elitist thinkers have consistently used this as an effective strategy to scapegoat, and to deny a helping hand to the less fortunate. A noticeable lack of concern toward the most vulnerable in our society, i.e. women and children however, should be more disquieting to people than it actually is. In the book we are reviewing, the point was made that childhood poverty has always been much higher in families headed by a single female, so the higher the proportion of children who live in these households, the higher the number of children who will live in poverty. However, to constantly suggest that single women with children in this country are immoral or somehow inferior because they are unmarried, less intelligent, or don't have a "legitimate" partner is ludicrous and simply not provable. And yet, the reasons why so many American males abdicate their responsibilities are never discussed.

It is also true that the different political parties disagree as to causes and therefore as to the policies that need to be created, however there have been creative and promising ideas that have been ignored and circumvented by those with a different agenda. In Reaganomics, ignoring the poor was referred to as *benign neglect,* and it remains a political maneuver to continuously avoid the poverty and deprivation of so many Americans. In this case, blaming the victims is replaced by ignoring them.

Moreover, we contend here that *misogyny* plays an integral part in domestic violence, sexual abuse the mistreatment of women, discriminatory employment practices, unfair and unequal wages, as well as being a factor in separations and divorce. Misogyny begins with mankind. Sadly, this troglodyte behavior has only been modernized and it crowds our courtrooms with its residual effects. It is deeply ingrained and often misunderstood as something outside ourselves. What graphs and charts don't tell us is that misogyny is not just attributed to those with limited intelligence and cognitive ability, and much like alcoholism and other disorders, it crosses, racial, social and economic lines affecting people from all walks of life. It is even found in women themselves, who succumb to a long history of patriarchal indoctrination and who sadly "know their place."

In the dictionary *misogyny* has been defined as the hatred and mistrust of women. What we've learned from studies in history, mythology and psychology is that misogyny also includes a fear of the feminine in general. American males have always held a belief that the female is the weaker and more inferior sex. When the Hebrew tribes settled around the Near East, they brought with them their own patriarchal sky gods. At the time however, the dominant deities were goddesses. Even the great tributaries were given feminine names, like the Nile, the Tigris and Euphrates, the Ganges. When these territories were invaded, the goddesses were condemned and eradicated for the most part. The Bible itself called women "the abomination," while depicting woman as being made from a man, Adam's rib. And to that, television sitcom character Archie Bunker smugly remarked that women were just made from a "cheaper cut."

Famous Greek philosophers even declared that women were not to be trusted; they had no souls; that men should worship god and women should worship men. We also know through the study of symbolism that the fear and hatred of the feminine is tantamount to a fear of the unconscious, so this does not appear to be a problem that will only be solved with outer solutions. And yet the same behavior has occurred over and over without a consideration for an **inner** balance of the masculine and feminine, that we believe begins in the human psyche. Materialism has been instrumental in teaching us that all the answers are to be found "out there," so the madness and the confusion continue.

So when looking at the reasons why women always seem to be treated as *less than*, we should strongly consider the age-old concept of misogyny, whose psychological and historical roots run deep.
We would even propose that the deep-seated fear and loathing of women may be one of the most dangerous and insidious problems facing us today. We're also learning that those places that are most affected by misogynistic behavior are (predictably) the places that are most likely to experience war and violence.

Obviously, the Bell Curve was written prior to the *Me Too Movement*, but the widespread mistreatment of women has been understood since before the *Suffragette Movement*, and yet women are still dealing with misguided political, social and economic policies -along with the despicable male behavior of the present. The wisdom of the activist and former first lady, Eleanor Roosevelt comes to mind as she encouraged women in their struggle to be treated with respect and dignity: "No one can hurt you without your permission."

Research by the authors also indicates that, at least among whites and regardless of intelligence, women who are unmarried and have no partner are more likely to experience poverty than women who have a husband. With all the talk in this society about love and marriage, should women then marry just to avoid poverty? Of course there will always be those whose primary concerns are for comfort and security. And, are unmarried men less likely to live in poverty, and if not, why?

There have always been women who were indoctrinated to be caretakers and housewives (**we** consider valued roles), while not being encouraged or supported to do other things. We also wonder how this impacts their lives after a divorce or a separation. And of course, as the authors noted, women of lower intelligence fair much worse economically than those with higher IQ scores. But with a total population of approximately 325 million, and over half of the population female, is this research an accurate representation of all single women and poverty in the U.S.? We will leave this assessment to the researchers.

And while the authors have given us some definitions of intelligence, at this point it is also important to distinguish between the terms "intelligence" and "cognitive ability" that are used interchangeably throughout the text. The *American Heritage Dictionary* simply defines intelligence as "the ability to acquire, understand and use knowledge," while its definition of "cognition" is "the mental process of knowing, including aspects such as awareness, perception, reasoning and judgment."

Having actually worked with low-income clients in a variety of settings, we can say unequivocally that unmarried women, and women in single-headed households, have for the most part shown themselves to be loving, responsible parents who do the best they can in very difficult situations, and with limited assistance from those who they rely upon for support. And a remark like, "...marriage is a powerful preventative to poverty…," whether accurate or not, only displays a bias against women who are not married for whatever reasons. This sounds more like a haughty suggestion for how women could avoid being poor. And while poverty may be a factor, this also fails to acknowledge that men of varying socioeconomic status and intelligence levels have chosen to walk away from their relationships on a regular basis. It should come as no surprise that in our male dominated society, reports indicate that the reason for the divorce rate not increasing (at around 50%) is due to the fact that women have become more reluctant to take the big plunge into the stormy waters of marital bliss.

Again, the current Me Too Movement clearly suggests that the mistreatment of women is still a pervasive problem in modern

America. We now know that it is also prevalent with men in positions of power and privilege, so maybe this could be the call for new and more accurate research into the matter. What we can propose is that misogyny itself is more of an unconscious process than one might suspect. After such a long history of such a pervasive problem, it seems that a new approach should be considered. "There is no chance for the welfare of the world unless the condition of women is improved. It is not possible for a bird to fly on only one wing." Swami Vivekananda

It is unfortunate that more data isn't available on these specific issues, but these are precisely the areas of concern that beg our attention. We would also like to take a moment here to make our own apologies for the use of the terms "man" and "mankind" when referring to humankind and the collective. It seems that even the language itself has been limited and one-sided when it comes to describing women and the collective.

In the end, what we lean towards is the notion that what is sorely needed is a paradigm shift in which we can acknowledge the need for a better understanding of what lies **within**. And a better understanding of the conscious and the unconscious psyche are vital to those ends. We clearly appear to be creatures of the opposites, and as such, we believe that the inner conflict people experience and those opposing forces, are a dynamic in our existence that is rarely considered. At this precarious time in our history we can only pose the question, "Can we can afford to leave any stone unturned?"

When the ancient stories and myths that permeate our movies, plays and literature are thought of as pure fiction, and merely entertainment, we miss out on their deeper lessons.

Throughout ancient mythology we see in its symbolism the stories of mankind, that have the ability to guide and teach us how to live our lives in ways that are not found through purely intellectual endeavors. They teach us how to live our lives on the inside. A deeper understanding is now in order.

A Basic Understanding

Before continuing our review of *The Bell Curve*, it is important for us to provide our brief description of this mysterious thing called the *unconscious*. We are all aware that it was first referred to as the *subconscious* by Sigmund Freud. It was his successor and protégé, C.G. Jung who referred to it as the *unconscious*, later naming it the *objective psyche*. Having touched on the subject earlier, we would now like to share a basic understanding of what we know so far. Understanding that supportive scientific data is relatively limited, we do have over a hundred years of empirical studies and clinical observations that can give us a basic outline.

1. As mentioned earlier, the human psyche appears to consist of two primary elements: the conscious "mind," of which we are most familiar, and the unconscious "mind," which is more obscure and often misunderstood. Freud considered unconscious content to exist below the level of consciousness, ergo his term *subconscious*, whereas Jung realized that the unconscious manifested itself in various ways in our conscious minds and in the outer world, e.g. we often hear about individuals who act unconsciously. It has been shown that people can also operate in a partially conscious state.

2. When this unconscious content emerges into our consciousness it becomes a personal matter where it becomes **our** psychic reality. It has also been observed that these images appear in dreams, fantasies and our imagination, and when they do, they more often appear in symbolic form. In many cases they can also carry powerful emotions. Who hasn't awakened from a dream feeling happy, sad or fearful and not have known why? Moreover, language, art, music etc. are all symbolic representations in their makeup. Through studies in symbolism and mythology, we also know that the unconscious is generally associated to feminine symbols, while the conscious psyche is represented by masculine imagery.

3. It is believed that consciousness needs and interacts with the unconscious, and that both are a necessary part of becoming a more whole human being. At the same time, the unconscious world seems to be expressing something that is beyond just earthly matters, something that might be considered spiritual. While these studies are empirical, they do not exclude *spirit* and *spirituality*. And although there are

phenomena that do occur outside the natural world, we understand that to use the term *supernatural* is vexing to some in the scientific community and to those who have been immersed in the scientific approach. We believe that those who hold so rigidly to a one-sided approach to life may eventually run into the wall of consciousness themselves, where going any further becomes extremely difficult.

4. Much like human beings, the conscious and the unconscious are found to be interconnected and interrelated. The unconscious appears to work in a compensatory fashion as it strives to bring consciousness into balance. In referring to a balance of the opposites, the renowned Danish physicist, Neils Bohr introduced the *Compensatory Theory* into the field of physics, which was also shown to have other applications. When he received the honor of the Danish Order of the Elephant in 1947, it was not by chance that he chose the Latin words *Contraria sunt Complementa* ("Opposites are complementary.") for his coat of arms. For his insignia he chose the Chinese symbol of the *Tai-gi-tu*, the intertwined opposites of the *Yin and Yang*, where each different half of the symbol shares a bit of the other's color.

5. As mentioned, it has also been observed that the unconscious element of the psyche can work more independently of consciousness. For those who believe that the conscious mind is in total control, it is difficult to accept that there is a part of our minds that could operate autonomously, however they need to review all the documentation that might show otherwise. There is phenomena around us all the time that remains unexplained by conventional science. This doesn't make it any less real. It was Jung who spoke of just how surprised people become when they discover that they are not the masters in their own house.

These concepts are sometimes difficult to apprehend and it is understandable that, even though these things have been observed over and over, the theories have mostly been ignored. They are not new to Analytical Psychology, which has its roots in the work of Freud and Jung and may be in part, the reason that these studies have been referred to as Depth Psychology. It plumbs the depths of the psyche beyond its conscious elements, as well as beyond the personal unconscious aspects. In the end, the unconscious may not fully be explained by science, but neither can it be explained away.

Family Matters

Moving on to the next section of the book, we take a little different look at family and marriage to consider other factors. Since most families begin with couples and relationships, our emphasis is on this core element. And while those with high IQ's often marry partners of similar intelligence, it is just as likely that other variables may come into play that might bring them together, or break them apart. It is also common knowledge that the length of a marriage does not determine the quality of that relationship.

And while this may not have been an area of concern for the authors of the Bell Curve, it is within our scope to consider. For the rest of us it may be even more important to discuss some of the real and human issues that affect our intimate relationships and social institutions that have been a part of our traditions for such a long time. It may be reasonable to assume that some of us believe that intelligence is not the only factor in how we begin and how we conduct our relationships. These ideas are important to explore, as they help to build the very foundations of the family.

If we follow what we've learned from psychological observation, then most relationships begin in projection. We've already established that projecting is primarily an unconscious process. The initial attraction is very real, and it can even be accompanied by physical symptoms. We begin to feel like we've finally found our significant other, our soul mate. It is difficult to convince those who are caught up in the early stages of romance that what they are likely experiencing is projection. And while this is not to say that some level of love and closeness is not involved, we often seek what we lack in another. We see a part of ourselves in the other person. They then become one of the most important beings in our lives. A more detailed discussion involving love and relationships will follow.

Those who have had the vantage point of seeing family issues from a more humanistic view will attest to the fact that partnering and family relations involve a lot more than just how smart we are. And again, if as the authors propose, being married is the antidote to financial problems and other difficulties, then those families who are together wouldn't be plagued with the constant problems and marital discord that we witness daily in the media. Is it possible that marriage does not immunize people from the same human problems that unmarried people have to face?

When we fall in love, we can safely say that this is the projective identification that psychologists allude to. In our basic understanding of projections, we know that even though it is a natural part of our behavior, negative projections and complexes can wreak havoc in relationships. When we project onto our partners, whether it is positive or negative, we are usually unaware that the other has been assigned to carry a missing part of ourselves. This in turn creates a powerful, unconscious identification with the other, who can then become the carrier of our well-being. They can also quickly become our greatest threat.

We can now just begin to understand that we can easily project our own angry and fearful internal images onto another. On the other side of this phenomenon we can just as easily project our adoration and feelings of love onto another, often exalting **or** blaming them in a manner that they may not deserve. It has also been shown that when this unconscious content is brought into our conscious awareness, then it no longer holds the power it once did. This should give us all the more reason to strive to become more conscious. This behavior can be observed in a variety of relationships, and particularly in our most intimate relationships. It is here that we see the most unusual, erratic, and sometimes the most violent and unhealthy behavior. It has often been said that no one can anger us more than those who we love most, so it might behoove us all to have a better understanding of ourselves. While we agree that family **does** matter, we also know that just having information about something does not necessarily mean that we will do what's best, or follow what the knowledge teaches. Therein lies the rub -we might know what to do, but not always do what we know.

In families we find fertile soil for the development of this unwelcome behavior. As indicated in the book in question, there appears to be a deterioration of the family, as well as other cherished institutions. What needs to be emphasized here is that it's just not possible or realistic to demand that people get along, or force them to stay together. In a society that may now be facing a cultural revolution, stark changes are inevitable. Trying to hold on to old ideas and traditions from the past is like fighting to stay stuck. Those who believe in these institutions can certainly participate in them and hold them dear, but it's the health of those relationships that seems most important. The increase of separations, domestic violence and abuse, along with unhealthy relationships in general, should give us all a reason to reassess what we've been taught to believe.

As mentioned, we are all products of our past, and as such, we are more often directed by that past. It is ego inflation that would have us believe that we are in total control of our actions and behavior and that our big brains have all the answers. A hard and honest look around might suggest something much different. And while it is nice to be positive, it also is important to realize that it is not always possible to remain positive. In psychological parlance, attempting to remain positive is a symptom of the ego and cultural learning.

And while love is said to be the glue, healthy families also require openness, honesty and communication. Like our other important relationships, families can only be as warm and healthy and as the individuals in them, and sometimes, even love isn't enough. There is no problem-free perfection.

To venture even further and risk the ridicule of traditional science, we again look at that mysterious element of the psyche that has been called the *collective unconscious*. This layer of the unconscious, that is said to extend beyond our personal past, is most interesting. In clinical studies and observations made over time, people have often reported seeing in their dreams and fantasies, images which they had never seen or knew about before. When these images are connected to history and ancient myth the entire psychic experience can be amplified through symbolic interpretation, and applied to the life and experience of the dreamer. While this seems uncanny, these experiences are observed and documented by analysts all the time. An understanding of all this has an effect on all our relationships.

From Abraham Lincoln to Eleanor Roosevelt, and including a number of primitives, people have cherished and recorded their dreams. Dreams are not only the doorway to the unconscious, they may very well be the path to becoming whole and balanced human beings. In his biography, Lincoln's vivid dream foretold of his inevitable death. And adding a slightly different slant, Eleanor Roosevelt once stated that, "The future belongs to those who believe in the beauty of their dreams." And yet dreams are only thought of as a byproduct of the brain and are largely ignored. This is the equivalent of receiving an important letter that is unread and discarded.

The authors briefly mentioned that norms and values change over time and yet their work would have us regress to past attempts at controlling others' thinking and behavior. We are aware that the zeitgeist also changes and yet there are those who would have us follow unquestioningly and conform to their way of thinking, condemning and chastising those who dare to march to the beat of a different drum. A fanatical need to have others do as we do has without question brought much pain and suffering into the world. And fanaticism is about compensation for our own doubts and fears. What we find across the board is that change for many people is extremely difficult. When we talk about change here, we are talking about personal, **significant** and **meaningful** change. The Greek philosopher, Heraclitus once declared that "the only thing of permanence is change," which brings us back to studies of so-called primitives. It is in this research we find the term *misoneism*, which is defined as the hatred or fear of change or innovation. Even in modern times people are often punished and ostracized for going their own way.

The deep yearning for the acceptance and approval of the pack often overrides the need for reason and common sense. Often times, peoples' stubborn and intransigent ideas are more about what is going on inside of them, but selective hearing, denial and the need to be right can cloud one's judgment, and often to the detriment of others. In challenging places like Mt. Everest, documentarist David Breashears has lectured about the "willful disregard for negative information," and how this behavior, which looks a lot like denial, can have negative results. Data and statistics are subject to scrutiny and information changes. More often, we see what we want to see and hear what we want to hear. Even when the information tries to steer us in another direction, we may ignore it and end up putting ourselves and others in great peril.

And while families in America **do** matter, they continue to *have* to do more and more with less and less. If callous ideologues were truly concerned about families in this country, perhaps they would not facilitate self-serving policies that perpetuate poverty and despair, for the same families they profess to care about.

Love and Relationships

Continuing our discussion about issues that have a lot to do with family (and the author's concerns), like love and relationships, we have seen that following the sixties and seventies women became more invested in their plight. Again, beginning with the Suffragette Movement and early activists, from Susan B. Anthony to Eleanor Roosevelt, and from Women's Lib to the current Me Too Movement, women are quickly finding their voice with the old guard still trying to silence and impede them. But as Carlyle duly noted, "No lie can live forever." The old ideas about "keeping the little woman in the kitchen" are thankfully dwindling, but the main battle wages on. It is important to repeat that misogyny has deep and stubborn roots that will not be eliminated easily. Our ideas of the masculine and the feminine will also need to be carefully revisited.

Simultaneously, we also fight the ego's incessant desire for power and control. Women's boldness and courage have also spilled over into the sociopolitical realm where they are successfully participating in politics and business, which scares the hell out of those myopic traditionalists who would deny them real independence and hold them down. Men in our culture proudly proclaim that they love women, but they just don't understand them. We strongly suggest that maybe they should begin by trying to understand themselves. The masculine and the feminine clearly exist physically in both sexes (e.g. recessive hormones and chromosomes), but the misunderstood inner connection is the most vital union of all. The Greeks called this mysterious union the *heiros gamos* -the sacred marriage.

In keeping with our psychological view about the union of men and women being about something deeper, and something more than just vows and certificates, we share a story that emerged from the ancient Greek psyche. In a myth from Plato's *Symposium* the original beings were perfectly round, having four arms and four legs with one head that had two faces which pointed in opposite directions. These beings were said to have amazing intelligence and phenomenal qualities that rivaled the gods. Since this threatened the celestial status quo, the gods became angry and jealous. They approached the mighty Zeus with their dilemma and this resulted in the spherical creature being severed into two equal halves with a sword. One half was female and the other male. As the story goes, those two parts have been striving to reunite ever since. This is the symbolic story of a more spiritual union of the masculine and the feminine that goes beyond just an intellectual understanding.

The realization that a relationship might be more about friendship, parity and a spiritual bond, than about submission and a piece of paper is freeing, life-affirming and more realistic. Observation has shown us that the initial attraction (projections) that one feels when encountering another wears off over time; then the bloom is off the rose. If one hasn't found openness, honesty and meaningful communication then that relationship is over. Intelligence is helpful but I am personally aware of many therapists and counselors whose offices are filled with those shipwrecked souls who refuse to take on the responsibility of their own journey. I personally believe that the inner journey is the most important voyage that we will ever embark upon.

You see, in the end, love is for people who know who they are. Others may struggle and strive or just be fortunate enough to have a harmonic relationship, but nothing can be more beneficial to everyone involved than a person who truly knows who they are. Ancient Christian scholars have even declared that when you know yourself, you know God.

So when we speak so glibly about the importance of marriage and relationships, let's not forget that it's not that simple. We are not all alike and what we see, and how we see these issues, are subjective. Our past, our complexes, fears and insecurities accompany us to complicate matters further. The psychologist, Robert A. Johnson referred to the kind of lofty, high-minded love we see on movie screens as *divine love*. Realizing how unworldly divine love was, Plato once asserted that this kind of love "is better left for the gods." Johnson then referred to a more realistic form of love as ordinary, "stirring the oatmeal" love; nothing that is exciting and spectacular, but what we experience after the passion and the excitement subside. As mentioned, this is where openness and honesty come in. The passion may diminish over time, but the chores and the responsibilities go on, while the familiarity increases.

The idea of romantic love goes back to the 12th century and the time of the troubadours, where the French word "romans" later morphed into the modern term romance. It began in Albi, in the south of France, and it was rooted in the Cathar faith, and what was known as the Albigensian heresy. At that time marriages were usually arranged by families and sanctioned by the church. However, when we speak of romantic love in modern times, we are unwittingly referring to a time when love was a more idealized state and not thought of as something so physical. Today we sexualize most all relationships between a man and a woman and often confuse sex with love. The corporate media associates love with everything from cars to pizza. And although sexual intimacy can involve love, sexual activity does not always involve two parties that love each other. These personal choices are left to the individual, however some would say that the ideal situation is sexual intimacy with someone you love.

Whatever people choose to believe, more often than not, when people elect to have sex for pleasure alone they only satisfy a basic carnal desire, which can also degenerate into an addiction. We may choose to believe that sex for pleasure only is not a bad thing, but hedonism has always been frowned upon. We also know that relationships based purely on sexual pleasure usually prove to be shallow and short-lived.

The ideal love of yore was a courtly love (*cortezia*) that involved no sexual liaison. The errant knight would court his beloved, who was most likely betrothed to another. It was believed that any sexual intimacy would degrade the idealized relationship and lower it to a bestial level. So without delving further, we summarize by saying that our modern idea of romantic love stems from a time long ago, when women were idealized, but not objectified like they are today. While this may seem ridiculous to today's anxious paramour, it is the modern idea of romantic love that is outdated, resulting in constant heartache and scores of failed and unhealthy relationships. The idea that something that had felt so good could hurt so bad is never fully explored. After the breakup of a relationship, some would even callously advise us to just move on to the next one.

The outdated notion of romantic love is deeply ingrained in Western culture and is no longer serving its subscribers as well as they had hoped. Human love is the pragmatic and not so exciting reality that most people end up having, if they're lucky. This doesn't mean that the passion and the intimacy have to end. The projections that we've been talking about fade over time, and this is the time when a relationship often becomes a power struggle. It is also at this time when couples are given the opportunity to rediscover themselves and redefine their relationships. Romantic love makes for great movies, crime shows and high TV drama, but from Tristan and Isolde, Lancelot and Guinevere, to Romeo and Juliet, the ending is seldom happy. In fact, even on television, some of the real-life couples that seemed to be so perfect and loving at first, end up being another crime statistic or a 911 call. Outside observers always seem confused and in disbelief when they discover that their friendly, church-going neighbor was so abusive, or may have even been moonlighting as a serial killer.

So while marriage set out to be a positive institution, and in many cases still is, convention should not be the sole basis for people coming together and it certainly hasn't been the idealistic glue that keeps people together. And if it is just an institution that was established to propagate the species, then love wasn't even that important to begin with.

Whatever might be said about marriage, women should not be punished for being single, or for having children out of wedlock, when it takes two to tango. This existential reality may never be explained by way of intelligence testing and statistics. These complicated issues have no pat answer, simple truth or technological solution. Oscar Wilde once stated that, "The pure and simple truth is rarely pure and never simple." However, when we lose our compassion, our understanding and our humanity, then we lose all possibility for viable solutions that work for everyone.

Another factor to review here is that when projections evaporate, and they always do, and we are left with the human love we just spoke of, then this is what is usually referred to as "falling out of love." To misinterpret this as the end of the relationship is common, but this indicates that the energy in that relationship has changed and a considerable amount of work by each person will be required. Sometimes so much damage has already occurred that a reconciliation may not be possible. The laws of physics have taught us that energy changes and although it doesn't disappear, it is said to dissipate and change form. When this begins to happen in relationships, a forlorn feeling of being unloved occurs which can then cause one or both partners to turn their projections onto another person, and the futile cycle continues. This often occurs with the fantasy of being rescued or saved by someone else. Often times, turning to another happens with little self-reflection or self-scrutiny and the deeper issues are never considered.

Core to our ideas about relationships and choosing partners is the idea of loneliness. What is often involved is a driving need to be with someone. The traditional indoctrination has been that it is socially desirable to have a spouse, a dog, 2.5 kids and a white picket fence. We are then told that this leads to the "happiness ever after" featured in *Modern Bride* magazine and programs like *The Bachelor*. We're not taught what to do when the "happiness ever after" fails.

What we don't learn is that we can be caught in the throes of loneliness and that this can occur in the familiar marriage bed, as well as in a crowd of a thousand. So to simplistically suggest that people should be married or stay married, for any reason, is ludicrous and unrealistic.

What is even more difficult for lonely hearts to hear is that it is precisely when we are alone that we begin to discover who we really are. When nobody is around to help; when mom and dad aren't there anymore; when we're thrown against our own resources, we are actually in a better position to find ourselves. In men's groups we've taught that if you can't be alone, then you can't be together.

In ancient lore, sojourners would venture into the desert or the wilderness to be alone and therein discover something vital about themselves -within themselves. One of the great stories in ancient mythology is precisely about this journey that one can bravely embark upon, called *The Hero's Journey*. Many of the great masters are said to have taken this journey at some point in their lives (e.g. Christ, Buddha, Muhammad). And it is only upon the leaving, the fulfillment and the return, whereupon the master is truly initiated and then experiences life in an entirely new way. The other element that is seldom talked about is that this usually involves suffering. And although it is difficult to hear, an effective approach to growth and healing is to understand that the only way out of the pain is through it.

When people choose a partner or spouse based on loneliness and neediness there is usually a price to pay. Afraid of being alone, people will often venture from one partner to the next, particularly after a breakup, but they never seem to find what they're searching for and they never seem satisfied. And some will stay in an unhealthy relationship because of a fear of being alone or a fear of change. This is when life can become very stressful and very wearisome.

Science and traditional wisdom do not teach us that when we embrace our loneliness we are in a position to turn that loneliness into solitude. And it is in our solitude that our own uniqueness is allowed to unfold, creating true individuality. Einstein himself once shared his own epiphany regarding the matter: "I now bask in that solitude that was so painful to me in my youth." The paradox is that it is precisely when we don't **have** to be in a relationship and don't **need** someone in our lives, that we are actually ready for someone. In a fun-loving, feel-good culture, solitude is undervalued and relationships are overrated.

Some people believe that they might lose themselves to another in a relationship. This only happens when we don't have ourselves to begin with. Some have even said that intimate relationships and having children may be the most difficult tasks of our lives. And some scoff at romantic relationships that end up "just" being friendships. However, when the embers of passion die and the thrill is gone, no amount of intelligence, money or talking can bring back the love that was lost. The love that appears to endure is the mutual friendship that was just made light of earlier. This may also involve trusting and allowing ourselves to be vulnerable, which can prove to be difficult for those who have been betrayed, abandoned or abused. True friendships and intimacy replace our ego's desires and take us beyond our ego needs, selfishness and insecurities so that we might at last experience something real and human.

To accept the thorns with the rose is to truly fathom that only the love is perfect, and not the people in it. While there is much more that can be said about this thing called love, suffice it to say that no amount of statistics and intelligence can adequately bring us to a better understanding. And neither will the accumulation of data be able to effectively direct the course of marriage, families or the complicated relationships within them.

Perhaps we should entertain other ideas when attempting to analyze families and dictate the policies that affect so many of us so deeply. As mentioned, it is possible that those with higher IQ's may remain together to maintain appearances, hold on to positions or social status, or even to preserve their finances and material wealth. It has also been observed that sometimes it is far easier to remain in a dependent or unhealthy relationship than to venture out into the cold, unpredictable world on our own. Since we are the progeny of our past, when the right situation arises, complexes are triggered and we react, conscious of it or not. My personal mantra is that I would rather be in no relationship than be in a false or unhealthy one.

The fact remains that we all have intrusive thoughts on occasion, and when these ideas are powerful enough, they tend to supplant will power. Sometimes these obsessive ideas are partially conscious and sometimes they operate independently. Of course the lack of control usually creates anxiety and is immediately followed by a reflexive behavior (e.g. smoking, drinking, gambling, etc.) which is actually meant to quash those anxious, unsettling feelings. More often, those feelings are only temporarily stifled, and when not addressed properly they will return to start the cycle all over again. So in any discussions about what individuals, couples and families should do, we can never forget the multifaceted problems and issues that can arise. After all, even ivy league graduates succumb to the unconscious forces that they may dismiss, but cannot avoid.

Families, couples and the human bonding and intimacy that are interwoven, are not solely defined by education levels, cognitive ability or income. Those relationships in which these issues become primary tend to lack in something that could be considered as more valuable. In a culture where marriage is said to be based on love, this can get complicated. In other places traditions differ, and yet those traditions might actually be more pragmatic than what is followed in the West.

In the East for instance, couples do not base their relationships solely on misguided passion that only fades over time. Their pairing is based on more practical reasoning. And like some arranged marriages, those unions often last longer than the Western relationships that are steeped in romantic love. Firmly planted in our own traditions and our way of life, we can't heal a Western wound with an Eastern remedy. While yoga and meditation are wonderful and useful practices, the philosophies and beliefs of the East go back centuries, and the psyches of those in the occidental societies are deeply planted in the Western ideas that dictate societal laws and norms, and direct our behavior.

One way in which the East/West dichotomy might be viewed is that in the East, their philosophy tends to transcend the ego. In the West, our reality relies heavily on the ego. In fact, while it may be hard to admit, the professional counselor, as well as the layman are beginning to understand that *ego inflation* is the dis-ease of our modern culture. Usually, the dangerous and unhealthy condition of *self-alienation* follows thereafter. In the end, we discover that the healthiest, loving and lasting relationships are those in which both parties are more balanced and content within themselves. Love is yet another complex human mystery that seems to defy quantification, or any other intellectual understanding. We are but instruments of it.

If there was a genuine concern for families, then we might be concerned enough in educating those individuals, and providing them with the knowledge and information that is required to create and maintain healthy relationships, and a cohesive family unit.

Divorce and IQ

In a subsection of the book entitled *Divorce and IQ* (pp. 174-177) the writers attempt to correlate divorce and intelligence. As with other areas of focus, IQ plays a primary role in how their remarks are made and their conclusions are drawn. Based on what is observed in the world of counseling and therapy, some of our decisions aren't always made so consciously or so intelligently. Romantic love has become such a powerful and popular phenomenon, and Westerners arrogantly assume that they have the best version of it. However, we're now discovering that much of what passes for romantic love in the West is psychological projection. We're also finding that a lasting love is supported by being attentive to the inner partners that reside in each of us, which gives us reason to consider a more psychological perspective. We have to proceed carefully here because those who are intransigent about their beliefs can quickly become upset when their ideas of love **or** religion are brought into question. It is said that the greatest enemy of truth is certainty.

In the field of marital counseling, a common refrain of some partners goes something like, "I thought I knew him (or her)." Most likely, they didn't know the other and probably didn't know themselves either. So when the authors hypothesize that "bright people less often marry on a whim...," this seems to defy life experiences and what we know about love and projections. It also demeans those people who may have scored lower on an IQ test, but may have also chosen to marry on the same whim as their more intelligent counterparts.

Las Vegas is crowded with couples who seem to leave all intelligence aside and make decisions for a lifetime based on an impulse or the thrill of the moment. Some long-term research could help us find out just how many of these marriages last. In the same paragraph we find the statement, "Bright people are less likely to act on impulse when the marriage has problems," although "less likely" is not a statement of fact. And in the very next statement we read, "More generally, it may be argued that brighter people are better able to work out differences that might otherwise destroy a marriage."

First off, we must ask ourselves if the statistics presented have actually substantiated all the conclusions. Examining these remarks further we suggest that impulsiveness or a lack thereof is not commensurate to intelligence. And while intelligence might be helpful, impulsiveness (i.e. "a whim") is not necessarily an inherent quality of people who may be less intelligent. In fact, impulsive and neurotic behavior in therapeutic settings are seen frequently within the ranks of those who are considered more intelligent and can more often afford therapy. While some behavior may be improved with the use of knowledge, it does not prevent people from acting badly. Notice any couple anywhere when they are arguing and fighting, and watch how quickly reason and intelligence flee the room.

However the statistics might be interpreted, most of these remarks could certainly be considered as offensive and insensitive. Again, the dominant theme of this controversial volume is the inference that people of higher intellect are just far more superior than those who are less intelligent. Many have suggested that the firestorm created by this book was its intention and that the surviving author is attempting to revive these themes at the most opportune time for divisiveness and more policy changes. We will leave this criticism for the readers who may also be wondering why, after all these years.

It is our firm belief that ordinary people of average intelligence may see each other as fellow human beings, with no person being better than another. This also seems to be in keeping with the teachings of great spiritual leaders like the Christ, who not only refused to discriminate between people for any reason, but rather, taught his followers to love and help those who were less fortunate and to even love their enemies, no matter their intelligence level or the color of their skin.

Sometimes, it's not so much what you have, as how you use it. In fact, if the authors of the Bell Curve are correct about the importance of cognitive ability, then those with power and superior intelligence must bear some responsibility for the global crises that we are now facing. The open denial of global warming and poverty by our elite leaders is a reflection of the denial and avoidance of their uninformed and misguided supporters.

This extends into all facets of life to include the disparity and inequality displayed in the way in which women and minorities are treated in the justice system and the workplace. In professing to believe in freedom, justice and equality it is interesting to note that when it comes to meting out punishment for crimes, the more affluent always seem to fare better than those of lesser means. Apparently, those with more intelligence and more resources, hold more value for some than those with less. The lyrics of an older pop song capture the sentiment: "A man with a briefcase can steal more money than a man with a gun," and we now see greed and corruption on an unprecedented scale. Some of our top business and political leaders are said to epitomize just how much crime pays, and they are considered to be the elites of our society.

In another segment of the book pertaining to *Family Matters* (p. 186) some controversial statements are made that might also help to explain the uproar about the book. While writing about poverty, welfare and IQ, we find comments about women in poorer communities who are considered irresponsible for giving birth out of wedlock. Here, the authors have justified their use of an early twentieth century term "illegitimacy," thereby subtly condemning an entire group of women for birthing children, no matter their individual circumstances. And it is also here that we can detect a personal bias that is attached to their otherwise more "objective" statistics.

Until further research is conducted, how can one know how many of these unwed mothers chose to be unmarried, and for what reasons? How can we know that the cause of their being unmarried was not due to the irresponsibility and lack of commitment by their male partners, or even abuse? The writers appear to choose the more pejorative terminology based on the thinking of a conservative anthropologist that they chose, and a questionable theory called the "universal social law," which then leads to the term "the principle of legitimacy." These and other terms were favored by the authors and used over more sensitive phrases like "out of wedlock births" and "births to single women." The use of this terminology is a subjective choice, as in the end, it is individuals that should determine whether something is acceptable based on their own knowledge, as well as their own conscience. This has been referred to as the freedom to think for yourself, where gaining more objective knowledge about issues might be more important than just accepting whatever the so-called experts may tell us.

Even more remarkable is the pronouncement that women with lower IQ's are likely to be unwed mothers in poverty simply because they are dumb and immoral. They assert that "...affluent young women are restrained by these moral considerations." While this is presented as fact, the moral level of these affluent women has not been established. The authors have not provided us with a direct link from poverty and their "dullness" euphemism, to immorality. In the real world we see a number of affluent women who display little compassion, sensitivity or common sense. We can only assume that in place of compassion and financial assistance the authors would prefer the persecution and banishment of these more unfortunate human beings. And we're still searching for the evidence that affluence somehow equates to morality.

As far as children born out of wedlock are concerned, the brighter minds that have prevailed so far have been instrumental in cutting sex education (and education in general) in the schools, disallowing discussions about abortion and unwanted pregnancies; even punishing some institutions for teaching birth control. What level of intelligence is employed here when the world now faces the serious problem of overpopulation? Some reputable critics have charged that the work we're reviewing might be skewed or interpreted for special interests. It seems as though there have always been certain groups that have targeted the weaker and less powerful members of our society, and the examples abound. Just one attack on women trapped in these disadvantaged situations is *The Moynihan Report*, published in 1965, which pathologized black unwed mothers. The scientific view of our world certainly has its value, however, when research is coupled with a lack of compassion and objectivity, it can encourage a punitive approach to sensitive issues. People can become angry and vindictive, and ever so willing to impose harsh laws and rules that scapegoat and punish others seen as inferior, based on the ideas and opinions of others. This is also accompanied by their own lack of a deeper self-knowledge.

Conflict and Competition

The first open war on poverty and the welfare system began with "the darling of the nation's conservatives," Ronald Reagan, who openly expressed his disdain of welfare recipients, and who believed that these needy louts were all "cheats and freeloaders" who should be forced back into the labor market (Trattner, 1974). It is now well known that Reagan, his punitive policies, and conservative mean-spiritedness in general, were greatly inspired by the white-identity politics that was later reinforced by dark tomes like *The Bell Curve*. The conservative movement was more than eager to welcome any theory or "research," no matter how erroneous or odiferus, to support their obsessive desire to prove others inferior and "less than."

Following the efforts of more benevolent leaders like Roosevelt and later Kennedy, the relentless attack on the poor and minorities continues to this day, with the needs of the wealthy always seeming to be of much more importance to politicians. When criticized and ridiculed about his concerns for the poor, Roosevelt responded with, "I welcome their hate." On a personal note, I have always been amazed about how those with so much could hold such animosity and disdain for those with so little. Could it be possible that wealth and intelligence do not equate to happiness or morality?

The intellectually contrived tactic of "blaming the victim" shows no signs of subsiding with its end results being a dramatic increase in poverty, crime and violence, as well as drug and alcohol abuse. Following another callous decision, Reagan's policies of *deinstitutionalization* saw scores of people released from mental institutions where they were thrown back out into the community with little or no resources or support. In a lack of understanding, or just a lack of compassion, no thought was given to just how many of these unfortunate souls might be incapable of caring for themselves. These voiceless victims now comprise a large majority of that ever-increasing group of expendable people called *the homeless*. And in all this, no attention has been given to the unnecessary and unfair practice of *corporate welfare,* which continues to give handouts to the unfortunate wealthy, while the rest of us are made to compete for less and less.

In an attempt to level the playing field, a *social safety net* was put into place, however more conservative thinkers have torn at the threads of any well-meaning plans to assist those in need. It appears that social change is influenced by the shifting relationships and interests of various groups competing for their own advantage. Any of these social issues involve some people who stand to gain, and some who stand to lose. No social process can be fully understood without referring to this conflict of interest. And the outcome of this conflict always favors the stronger (richer) party. In American society, particular interest must be paid to the interests and values of those who exercise power. In America those people have historically and primarily been white, middle-aged, wealthy, Protestant males of Anglo-Saxon descent. Behind their chosen leaders and the middle class facade are the wealthy puppeteers. Once this power structure has been established then it is extremely difficult for them to relinquish that power or to have them concede to any wrongdoing.

While it is vital to have an understanding of the monopolization of power in this country, it is important to remain vigilant about various groups with their own self-interests in mind. At this time it is particularly important to mention *The Federalist Society,* that has been working surreptitiously behind the scenes to buy and control our government. Following decades of disdain for democracy and equality, this quiet group of elitists has worked feverishly to push forward their self-serving agenda. Along with a few other groups mentioned throughout our volume, these are the puppet-masters that pull the strings. They have clearly been moving us toward their self-made artificial paradise, where only they will partake in abundance and prosperity, and the fruit of **our** labors.

The conflict perspective that we described emphasizes consensus and stability, but it so narrowly focuses on competition and progress that it misses the more stable, orderly and less conflictual dimensions of social reality. And consensus, stability and the will of the people are becoming less and less of a concern for these elitist leaders, who care only about their own social reality.

In lesser known research done by a group of psychologists, using several groups of school-age children, it was discovered that mutual cooperation was far more effective than competition in creating productive and cohesive behavior with the children in those studies. While the studies may have been relatively limited, the results were clear. There was much less fighting and bickering, and the children in the less competitive groups actually enjoyed working together. It's also obvious that competition can breed aggression, distrust, envy, divisiveness and the need to win at all cost. In competition, someone always has to lose in order for someone else to win. In America no one likes a loser, but not everyone can be a winner. Mutual cooperation puts much less emphasis on winning and is more about people helping each other and working together towards a common goal. Competitiveness and one-ups-man-ship have had a damaging effect on families, business, politics and every other aspect of life.

As far back as 1992 competitive U.S. businesses had spent over one trillion dollars on marketing alone, convincing people to buy more and more. This spending obviously resulted in the profit increases that have only supported the interests of corporations, who recruit the best minds that money can buy in order to sell us more. We contend that the new gods of Profit and Gain have led to the greed, emptiness, loneliness, and self-alienation that have become commonplace. Unsurprisingly, these afflictions seem to affect those who have it all even more.

The above mentioned amount far surpassed the sum spent on education at the time, which amounted to about $600 billion. This included private and public education at all levels. The great sociologist, C. Wright Mills called on a resistance to the greed and corruption through the form of "a far-reaching moral resolution." In order to accomplish this, he suggested we needed to confront what he called the "higher immorality," a "structural immorality built into the institutions of power in our society." Going further he wrote, "In a civilization so thoroughly business-penetrated as America, money becomes the most unambiguous marker for success...the sovereign American value." (Crooks & Stein, 1988)

A society dominated by the corporations and the rich, with the full support and protection of the political elite, becomes a society of "...organized irresponsibility, where moral virtue is divorced from success, and knowledge from power" (Danaher, 1996). Author and activist Rachel Carson (*Silent Spring*) denounced the corruption, pollution and destruction of our environment in the sixties, and then described the time as "an era dominated by industry, in which the right to make money, at whatever cost to others, is seldom challenged."

With everything being relative we fast-forward to the present where we have seen the education system turned on its head. In 2018 we saw the federal government and the current administration slash the budget for education, with plans to slash billions more. While we can only speculate on what the future may bring, we can only wonder about the level of intelligence being used to make these seemingly thoughtless decisions. Moreover, we would ask what all the people of superior intelligence are actually doing themselves to avert a potential social crisis and provide everyone with the equal opportunity to an education.

A more educated society can only be detrimental to those who choose to see it as a threat.

Throughout the text the authors continue to express their deep concern for intelligence and education, however the politicians and business leaders who they support, and who support them, do not appear to be acting in the best interest of ordinary people. We cannot remain naive about how damaging this really is. The corporatization of the American education system has become obvious, and along with it is what has been called the dangerous rise of academic capitalism, accompanied by the dramatic decrease of academic freedom.

It is quite clear that poverty, along with racism and misogyny are built into the system. We also know that the long-term campaign for elitist supremacy is an unending and central part of the plan. Blaming the victim is not a new concept, however, combined with a lack of integrity, fair-mindedness and compassion, darker forces win out. Some researchers have estimated that in the wealthiest country in the world, one out of every four children lives in poverty and the numbers are rising. We lament because these children are vulnerable and innocent victims who have done nothing to deserve such a fate. And it seems pretty clear that the children are not our future, we are theirs.

Parenting

While it is correct to conclude that "...how well parents raise their children has much to do with how society functions" (p. 204), this may present an incomplete picture in explaining just how society functions at large. And while cognitive ability relates to parenting, there are a variety of ways in which people parent their children. This line of research has not taken into account the fact that children are individuals with different inherent abilities, and there are some children who just don't do well in a school setting. We all know that children learn differently, and what works for one may not work well for the other. So again stressing that we are all products of our parents and our past, other factors appear to play in when it comes to the learning process and parenting habits.

For instance, does this line of inquiry take into consideration abuse and mistreatment by the parent, or stress experienced within the family at home? This definitely has an impact on how a child learns. Are younger children provided with proper food and nutrition? This has also been shown to affect the child's attention and learning ability. This, along with poverty, are a major concern of educators across the country, where proven programs like *Head Start* and even school lunches have recently come under attack by conservatives, who continue to ignore the major impact of poverty on children. In fact, there have been several reports of teachers taking money from their own pockets to provide children with needed school supplies. We're still waiting to hear from those higher intellects, and those champions of education.

Experience has taught us that parents who live in poverty do not always learn the value of education and so in turn do not always teach that value to their children. They are usually indoctrinated with the old work ethic, where their hard work is often proven to be more beneficial to others. Each member of society functions on the attitudes and values acquired as they grow up. If my parents display prejudice and animosity towards people of color, then it is likely that I will mirror their behavior, without ever challenging the logic and fairness of that thinking. What is overlooked, are the personal and intrinsic qualities that a parent or a child may already possess.

This may also involve an inner darkness that they are not fully aware of, and whether their own ethical standards of right and wrong prevail. If I am taught that the important thing in a society is to amass money and things, then I may become susceptible to a more materialistic mindset. I might also choose a path that is more generous and benevolent. This all has less to do with IQ, and more to do with the vital role a parent plays in mirroring behavior. Harder to accept, is that it is also a reflection of the deeper core within. And usually, parents cannot give what they weren't given. This alone should encourage a more supportive attitude towards those parents who have to do more with less.

Whatever their status, when parents display erratic or unhealthy behavior as a young child is growing up, we know that this has a definite impact on the child later in life. The child simply cannot assess that "...my parent is acting poorly (or having problems), and this has nothing to do with me." We know that children observe the way parents handle issues and react to situations, and that they not only internalize that behavior, but they also assume adaptive behavior that can prove to be unhealthy. Watching how their parents navigate through life has a powerful influence on how children see the world and how they see themselves in it. As parents, we may try to educate, control and discipline our children as best we can, but all the IQ and knowledge in the world may not produce the outcome that we desired. It's also evident that there are no such thing as perfect parents, and that there are only good enough parents.

In addition to these complications, when parents can't "let go" of a child and create a dependency, or attempt to live vicariously through the child, then this also sets up the child for problems down the road. It is of paramount importance for children to break away from parents physically **and** psychologically. This does not mean that children must separate from their parents completely, however enmeshment with a parent can be detrimental to the child's development and independence. Some grown children, who've moved away from home, phone their parents every day and this does no service to the growth and autonomy of those children. And while it was not intended to demean parents, analyst C.G. Jung once wrote that parents "should always be conscious of the fact that they themselves are the principle cause of neurosis in their children." (Wickes, *The Development of Personality, CW 17*)

Even with the importance granted to intellect and the statistical data on parental IQ, to ignore the possibility that deeper psychic processes are involved is to have only a partial understanding of human behavior. Several children may be raised in the same household and turn out differently. It is always disconcerting when children who are treated well in a home, surprise their parents with behavior that is troubling and even harmful.

When the authors proclaim that "Child abuse in some bizarre forms has nothing to do with anything besides a profoundly deranged parent," this only displays the authors' lack of understanding human behavior. Abusive parents come in all varieties, rich and poor, intelligent and less intelligent, and most are not insane, let alone "profoundly deranged." We also know that when children are abused, they tend to become abusive adults themselves. Television programs and documentaries overflow with the stories of "ordinary" middle class children who commit serious crimes, to include murdering their own parents, which can sometimes lead back to the parents' behavior. While there is a case for malparenting, this does not exclude parents who are on a higher rung of the socioeconomic ladder. The high TV ratings on many of these popular shows come by virtue of the fact that everyone is fascinated by how such an upstanding, successful family could have produced such a monster. This type of unhealthy behavior among the more prominent members of society may be indicating a trend that deserves more attention.

Again, while there may be a correlation between malparenting and socioeconomic class, it is the biased and condescending tone of the remarks that taint the authors' conclusions. In this same segment, while defending their position on malparenting and class we read, "The people who argue otherwise do not offer data to make their case." While studies have been conducted that disprove these old ideas, some of these issues require only experience and common sense to understand. With one sentence the authors attempt to disregard any arguments that are not based on their research. This is followed later in the volume by condescending arguments that make it seem as if theirs was the only opinion that mattered. When you speak loudly and drown out differing opinions this doesn't make what you're saying any more valid or true. We also know that at the time of its publication there were many researchers that successfully refuted the book's premise. The dust seemed to have settled, until a recent resurgence of mean-spirited thinking breathed new life into a frozen corpse. We can rest assured, that while millions suffer, a generous spending of resources will provide us with new information to convince us that the poor and the voiceless are still not deserving of our help. We spend our time and money on that which we value most.

In finishing our thoughts on this section we can only say, without the flood of statistics, that a humanistic approach simply suggests that parenting and human life itself are more complicated. They even involve a psychological element that data alone has not been able to help us understand. We firmly believe that with a little different thinking and a deeper understanding of the human psyche, we may be better able to achieve balance and harmony in many areas.

With all the advantages and opportunities that more privileged families obviously have, then by their own standards, there is no justification for their own damaged children. Waiting rooms are filled with the collateral damage created by the parents who have abdicated their responsibility to change themselves. It's much simpler, but less effective, to pay others to repair the damage afterwards. And in defense of all those imperfect parents, we contend that there is no such thing as an infallible parent, and that in reality, we will be defined by the goodness and decency that is displayed by our children and what we've left behind. Though it may be unintentional, parents confer upon their children their own unsolved problems. And while intelligence is involved, this has less to do with test scores and more to do with how parents travel their own journeys and who they are as human beings.

Crime

Turning now to the section on crime, we work from a more practical perspective. More current and objective research would be in order. Data that is more inclusive of minorities and how the different ethnic groups are used in these studies might also be helpful. We also see a need to distinguish between the types of crimes that are committed and those types of criminals that might be committing them. The well-known attorney Clarence Darrow once exclaimed, "There is no justice, in or out of court."

For instance, we've seen no mention of the ever growing problem of white collar crime. This is also an issue that is not adequately covered in the mass media, and although an argument could be made that white collar crime is less prevalent than other types of crime, it costs us much, much more. And it has already been established by others that there are other factors that contribute to crime, like poverty, inequality, and less opportunity. We were not provided with data on the all-important variable of poverty, as it plays into every facet of social life. We hope that these factors are not forgotten when assessing the actual costs of crime.

Another much less discussed factor when speaking of white collar crime is the political ploy of *deregulation.* While prosperous corporations cry that they are hindered by unnecessary government regulations, their profits have soared exponentially over the last several decades. The checks and balances that had previously been put into place have been ignored and circumvented by lobbyists and special interest groups. Current financial experts predict another economic collapse in the near future, while the coffers of big business are overflowing.

It is more than obvious that corporate crime and corruption have contaminated every office of government, politics and the economy. With questionable tax loopholes and surreptitious offshore accounts, the rich are having a field day. One thing we can say with certainty, is that wealth and power addicts cost this country and this world far more than all the alcohol and drug-related crime combined.

The craving for power and money is not a new problem, however today's best thinkers are employed by think tanks and mass media to control information and manipulate the general public around these issues. Their arsenal is filled with the tools of control and manipulation: distractions, embellishment, labeling, re-framing, hyperbole, and mendacity are also used against us. Buying and controlling legislators and politicians also contributes to their incessant desire for more and more. And while people seem to understand all this, they are steered towards apathy and numbness by the constant distractions under the big top of the media circus.

It is important to point out that a restless and insecure ego is never satisfied, and that more will never be enough to fill these empty vessels. Attempting to fill ourselves with things outside ourselves is an effort in futility, but it seems far more important to some people than honesty, self-awareness and compassion. What needs to said here is that fear and insecurity play a big role in the minds of those who mistakenly equate having more with being more. And the endless media coverage of petty criminals far exceeds the coverage of the white collar crime that we should be focused on.

Sensationalism may be good for ratings but it contributes nothing to the solutions that are sorely needed in our society. The mass media contributes even more to the confusion by framing one group as the good guys, who must control and punish the bad guys -good over evil. This successfully divides the criminals and the suspects, from the other group who are portrayed as the heroes and the good guys. This effective method is now a common tactic for the corporate media that instills fear, violence, distrust and suspicion. An instrument that could be used to teach and unite is now a tool of divisiveness and fear-mongering.

Many believe that there is a thin line between a cop and a criminal, and that line has been crossed on a multitude of occasions. An interesting feature of crime and punishment is pointed out in a new book by Emily Bazelon (*Charged*), who proves irrefutably that in the past few decades, violent crimes have decreased significantly, while mass incarceration has dramatically increased. The book clearly reveals that the penal system is ineffective, unfair, costly and inefficient.

In our languid thinking, this situation may be viewed as "just the way it is, after all, they're only criminals," however our society continues to produce criminal types who will be released back onto the streets. The corporate media hammers us with programs that sensationalize crime and violence, while glorifying police and the military. This in turn desensitizes us to the violence and then allows the authoritarian system to proliferate. It's the old frog story: Put a frog in hot water and it will quickly jump out of the pot, but turn the heat up slowly and before it even notices, it's cooked.

The "tough on crime" stance is only a modernized version of the antiquated good over evil ideas and it usually sets up those in power as the good. Instilling fear and distrust, it normalizes an authoritarian state and paves the way for a very gloomy future. Of course evil exists, but evil can never be fully eliminated, and yet there will always be those who set themselves up as being the good, while projecting their own darkness onto others that they label as bad and undesirable. But as it was once said, when one man is not free, then no man is free. Meanwhile, the inane distractions continue to entertain us and keep us from the inevitable appointment with ourselves.

When speaking of evil, we must briefly mention that its close companion, hate gets little attention in attempting to understand the human darkness that is prevalent in all people, but seldom discussed. Some believe that the opposite of love is hate, while others hold to the notion that the opposite of love is not hate, it is fear. There are even those who have theorized that it is much easier to hate than it is to love. Either way, these are the deep-seated archetypal patterns of behavior that are commonly seen in the psyche. These are the very opposites that we must become aware of and deal with on an individual basis. This would put the burden and the responsibility for our own hatefulness squarely on each one of us. Aware of it or not, depth psychology tells us that we are inextricably linked to the things that we love, just as much as to the things we hate. While this certainly gives us something to think about, the caustic effects of hate and evil on the mind and the soul need no further explanation.

Awarded the Nobel prize for literature, the great Russian writer Aleksandr Solzshenitsyn once wrote:

"If it were only so simple! If only there were evil people somewhere insidiously committing evil deeds, and it were only necessary to separate them from the rest of us and destroy them. But the line dividing good and evil cuts through the heart of every human being. And who is willing to destroy a piece of his own heart."

The recent transference of wealth to the most affluent, behind the pretext of "tax reform" is testimony to a self-serving agenda, but the ongoing pillaging, which began on their watch, somehow went unnoticed by our authors. This dire situation certainly existed at the time of their writing. It is well known that the top 1% of the wealthiest Americans in the country now own over 90% of the wealth, and their wealth increases. What we are currently dealing with is nothing new and has been referred to as "the Return of the Robber Barons." Mark Twain once accurately described the American capitalist mindset: "Get money. Get it quickly. Get it in abundance. Get it in prodigious abundance. Get it dishonestly if you can, honestly if you must."

There are other statistics that exist that clearly show the legitimized crimes perpetrated on the American people in a trend that was set years ago. The Forbes 400, in just one example, stated that in 2002 the average wealth for the 400 richest Americans went up 409%. As far back as 1982 their assets went from $428 million to $2.18 billion in 2002. The average wealth of the poorest 80% of American families went up just 18% -in 1982 from $54,000 to $63,800 in 2002. And of course with recent "tax reform" and deregulation the gap is getting much wider. This is all legitimized by hiding behind the banner of *free market capitalism.*

In 1981, conservative Ronald Reagan, while signing the law to deregulate the savings and loan industry (eventually leading to an economic disaster) reportedly boasted, "I think we've hit the jackpot with this one." (Brouwer, 2004) Not only has the plundering continued unabated, but mass corruption and mendacity have received the Presidential Seal of Approval. We are confident in asserting that deregulation has only legitimized greed and corruption.

This capitalistic mindset, with the help of the elite, has also been exported overseas where well-funded organizations, along with the American military, will ensure the control and hegemony over weaker and more vulnerable countries. It looks like the most egregious crimes of the modern era are not committed by the poor, women or minorities, whose only crime has been in attempting to obtain justice, equality and dignity. They have constantly been thwarted by those more intelligent people who care nothing about unity, peace or equality. (We will be returning to crime-related issues as they arise.)

At this point in our discourse, it is vital that we understand that the mass media bears culpability when it comes to controlling and manipulating information, as well as disseminating misinformation and propaganda. This is not really a surprise, as it is owned by the same corporations and elitists that often hide in the shadows of power. Some critics have even labeled the news that we see as "info-tainment." Most of us don't see the journalistic value in a car chase, and quite frankly, critical thinkers don't care about the banal details of an empty celebrity's life. Maybe this is where a little intelligence could go a long way. This culture was once referred to as "the culture of divertissement," where the mass media competes to mesmerize us, drawing us further away from ourselves with the distractions of the moment. Their concerns are only about ratings and market share. Even the leader of the free world is a former game-show host.

The corporate media sells us our politicians and our President the same way it sells us our blue jeans and our cars. We shouldn't wonder why people are uninformed and misinformed, buying into the mindset of materialism and toxic consumerism. So when we speak of intelligence and how a society functions it would be remiss to forget that attitudes, beliefs and opinions can be shaped and manipulated. Politicians and the corporate media learned that the best way to control one group of people is to have them fear and distrust another group. The affluent also learned long ago that the way to manipulate the poor and the middle class is to have them want to be rich like them, regardless of their real-life situations.

As far back as 1938, E.B. White made a remarkable prediction when he stated, "I believe television is going to be the test of the modern world, and that in this new opportunity to see beyond the range of our vision, we shall discover either a new unbearable disturbance of the general peace or a saving radiance in the sky. We shall stand or fall by television -of this I am quite sure." Elitist thinkers who control mass media and information have made the choice not to be honest and more helpful. Their self-serving agenda speaks to a grim future for our children and for future generations. Considered the father of social psychology, Edward Alsworth Ross commented that, "A corporation is an entity that transmits the greed of its investors, but not their conscience."

The recently installed FCC Chair has given free rein to television networks, attacking public television, while turning his back on the protection of vulnerable viewers in our society. And it looks to be open season on taxpayers and consumers. And what are they teaching our children? In a classic study written some decades ago, entitled *Four Arguments for the Elimination of Television*, author Jerry Mander wrote, "Broadcast television is available only to monstrous corporate powers. What we are permitted to see on television is what suits the mentality and purposes of corporations." Corporations would not spend tens of millions of dollars on marketing and advertising if their shady strategies were not effective. We will not discuss in detail the reasons why so many people are easily swayed and convinced to buy things that they may not need. A short answer might include materialism, compulsivity, gullibility and those who prey on those weaknesses, paired with the indoctrination of the mass media at a very young age. So again, when talking about crime, social behavior and intelligence let us remember that it's not what we're told. And if meaningful and significant studies are to be done then let the research include the unhealthy behavior of those who are considered more intelligent and more affluent, and therefore, should be more responsible, and certainly more accountable.

Later in this section, comments are made inferring that criminals are psychologically and biologically deficient, but no real evidence has been provided. While education and intelligence may be a factor, other things that contribute to crime have not been considered. Using 19th century terminology the writers plant a powerful image in their readers' minds that chronic offenders may be suffering from "moral insanity" although insanity might necessarily exclude a sense of morality. Once someone is considered insane, how does being moral even fit into their actions and behavior? Insane acts seldom involve the perpetrator considering whether the act is right or good, the basic definition of morality. How are the authors correlating being moral to insanity here? It also seems to us that white collar crime requires more intelligence than those crimes committed by someone who is considered to be less intelligent. But how are the authors measuring the morality or the sanity of either group?

We welcome studies on the causal link between insanity and immorality that is presumed by the authors. This research might also include whether more intelligent criminals suffer from this same moral insanity. Or, if considered sane and intelligent, are their crimes just a case of a deficiency of ethics, where perpetrators know the difference between right and wrong but commit the crime anyway? It seems clear that just possessing wealth and intelligence is not an effective preventative for crime, malfeasance or immorality. And a clear definition of moral insanity has not been provided.

Looking further at their conclusions on crime, the authors promote the idea that there must be a biological cause for criminal behavior. This may have some validity, but a clear link to biology or heredity as a cause for criminal behavior has not been established. This conclusion may have been drawn to advance their theories on hereditarianism. By doing this, then it is much easier to extrapolate the criminal behavior of a few onto whole groups and entire families. Their conclusions would then suggest that criminal behavior must be transmitted in the same way that hair color and even creativity are (sometimes) acquired -biologically. More recently, after contrary research was presented, there has been more acceptance of the environmental components that have proven to be the larger factor.

We are all familiar with the documentaries about the precocious child, particularly in the field of music, who is a virtuoso at a very early age. The reason that these stories become so popular and compelling is because we perceive their talent to be premature or somehow special, for their age. We have then heard some of these same parents exclaim that they themselves had no musical ability. How is this explained by the scientific community? By adhering so adamantly to hereditarianism (which has its value) some researchers deny out of hand, the notion that there is a possibility that some human traits might come from something other than our genes. Much like fantasies and the other mysterious images that come through our imagination the idea is never considered that possibly, creativity doesn't come **from** the mind but **through** it. A bit of wisdom from the Eastern Philosopher J. Krishnamurti comes to mind here. "It is the activity of the mind that is a barrier to its own understanding."

Since we are coming from a psychological perspective, relevant to these thoughts is the etymological meaning of the word *psyche* itself from which words like *psychology* and *psychiatry* are derived. Of Greek origins, the word psyche has the original meaning of "soul" or "spirit." So from a psychological view this might suggest that these disciplines originated from observing something deeper, and not just seeing the brain as the only source of all mental activity. The notable physicist, Fritjof Capra once averred, "Science does not need mysticism and mysticism does not need science, but man needs both." (*The Tao of Physics*, 1975) The reductionistic view of science can no longer explain away the phenomena that is occurring all over, all the time. It seems that the arrogance of science is displayed in believing that it has the answers to everything. These bold attempts at discovery are useful and sometimes even admirable, but looking at the world today, that very technology that was developed to advance humankind is now haunting us in ways that were either ignored or unforeseen by those same brilliant minds that created it.

"Our scientific power has outrun our spiritual power. We have guided missiles and misguided men. Our hope for creativity lies in our ability to reestablish the spiritual needs of our lives in personal character and social justice. Without this spiritual and moral awakening we shall destroy ourselves in the misuse of our own instruments."   Martin Luther King Jr.

What is being ignored and misunderstood throughout is the very real unconscious element of the human psyche. Since our observations of the unconscious do not always agree with the scientific understanding of how the mind works, and since causality is not always applicable, their doubt is understandable. However, clinical experiences and an empirical approach to an understanding of the unconscious continue to reveal that the conscious mind does not operate alone. Psychologists and therapists in the field have never claimed to have all the answers and can only document and report how the unconscious acts and behaves. We again maintain that the unconscious can no more be fully explained or defined than consciousness. We propose that much like the notion of deity, it is an ineffable mystery.

In the following quote by Einstein, we believe that the word *spirituality* can be thought of as being interchangeable with the word *religion:* "Science without religion is lame and religion without science is blind." Much like the Capra quote earlier it seems that these great physicists are asserting that religion -or spirituality- and science are not mutually exclusive.

Our unconventional approach to understanding other aspects of the psyche was originated by Freud and Jung, where each made their own special contribution. Jung's unique and eclectic view respects the importance of science and the scientific approach, while believing in the need for a confluence of science and spirit, and it is more possible than one might think. His research and deeper understanding of the unconscious led to his estrangement from Freud, whose theories continued to overshadow those of his protégé. Unfortunately, within the limits of this volume, there is not enough time to fully detail the ideas and theories of these two great pioneers of the human psyche.

In addition, we also suggest that there are said to be other forms of intelligence, and that the world of spirit and soul cannot be dismissed so easily. Some modern scientists even claim to have religious beliefs -does this alter or discount their scientific observations and their research? The word religion has its etymological roots in the Latin words "religere" and "religare." The latter appears to be the preferred term used by many early theologians. *Religare* originally meant "to bind, or link back to." These meanings then lead us to other questions. The next thing we might ask is: "What are we linked or connected to?" What Analytical psychologists have theorized is, linked back to a deeper source inside of ourselves. We understand that this is really difficult for those disciples of scientific rationalism. And yet people in all corners of the globe have some type of religious or spiritual beliefs.

Returning for a moment to the topic of crime, we are faced with yet another motivating factor, some of which was touched on briefly by our authors. Since civilization began, our cultural ancestors the Greeks, understood the value of avoiding and even scorning *hubris* and *concupiscence* and this was carried out into early Christian thought. In our use of the word concupiscence we would like to point out that a strong desire does not only concern sex, and that the lust for money and power certainly fall within its scope. The Bible condemns these transgressions as serious offenses.

Successful author and prominent attorney, Gerry Spence consciously turned from a lucrative career, at first defending the malfeasance of corporations, to defending the victims of corporate crime. Two exceptional courtroom victories for Spence included the well-publicized Karen Silkwood case, as well as his impressive win over Ford Motor Company's best attorneys. In the latter case it seems that in their attempt to save $88 million by not adding an $11.00 safety device to their Ford Pinto at the time, an estimated 500 people were burned to death as a consequence of the car's exploding gas tank. So these needless deaths were caused by corporations who believed in profit over people. And yet this was considered more of a business risk than a sordid act or a potential crime by corporate America.

After careful thought and self-scrutiny Mr. Spence switched teams and through personal, anguishing experiences something deeper (and not necessarily religious) inside of him broke through and guided him in a different direction. This is just one real-world example of how our thinking may be guided by something more than just our cognitive ability. Paraphrasing from the book, Spence proclaimed that greed was a dangerous and contagious disease. And **we** believe, that those who are afflicted, are separated from the family of man. Aligned with our own ideas about both poverty and criminals, Spence declared, "We lock them up in cruel places. But we do not protect our starving children in this world from being murdered by the greedy." (*With Justice for None*, 1989).

It would seem that the more successful and intelligent not only commit serious crimes, but that their crimes often cost society and taxpayers in more than just dollars. There's also been much talk about how a double standard exists for those who commit white collar crime, as they receive less punishment for their infractions. They are usually sent to "country club jails," with much different treatment if they are ever convicted of a serious crime. Speaking about crime and incarceration, the U.S. currently has the highest rate of recidivism in its prisons, at around 80%. The country of Norway is currently at a 20% rate. Norway is mentioned, not only because of its comparably low recidivism rate, but because the reason for this has been attributed to their focus on genuine rehabilitation efforts. Costing taxpayers millions of dollars, the "jail industrial complex" continues on unabated. Profit-driven prisons sell shares on the stock market, so the more people they have incarcerated, the more profits they make. It is inaccurate to suggest that the criminal justice system is broken, because it's working -just as it was intended to. In a country where the new gods of Profit and Gain reign supreme, you get the kind of justice that you can afford.

Throughout the book we have been exposed to the authors use of data taken from the National Longitudinal Survey of Youth (NLSY). After reviewing Appendix 2, we found it difficult to determine just how many minorities were included within the chosen subjects, and how many people of color represented which ethnic groups. Having the disadvantage of not being scientists ourselves we could only wonder how different the outcome and interpretations might have been if a proportionate amount of minorities (to include women) were represented in the sample groups, particularly in relation to these various correlational studies.

As regards crime, there are various publications that have indicated that blacks and Latinos are disproportionately arrested, convicted and imprisoned in our judicial system. We did not find anything in the book that would help us understand the link between poverty, crime and minorities. We understand that there is a link between low IQ and criminality but precisely to what extent? Since we know that poverty exacerbates crime, drug use and violence, it's difficult to understand how little of this was even mentioned. Common sense might dictate that people with less resources and less incentives have less of a chance for education and opportunity, and so less of a chance for increasing their knowledge and improving their lives. The authors even state that "...the great majority of people with low cognitive ability are law abiding." (p. 251)

While the role of socioeconomic status is discussed, it appears that the sample groups used in some of these studies were primarily made up of white males, and some of the collection of data is gathered through self-reporting, which has the tendency to be limited in its accuracy. Excluding other variables and other possibilities keeps the continued focus on proving that IQ is the overriding factor when it comes to crime.

When our politicians and business leaders ignore and circumvent the issue of poverty, they only contribute to its dramatic increase, which is becoming more and more obvious in our country, where there are more people incarcerated than most other industrialized nations. Some say that there are sins of commission and there are sins of omission. Gandhi once declared that the greatest crime perpetrated on people was poverty. Recent giveaways to the wealthiest of the wealthy, along with providing billions to an already bloated military budget are true indicators of an agenda that no longer serves those of us who actually foot the bills. Those who support what Dr. King referred to as "the madness of militarism," display concerns only for dominance, wealth, power and destruction. But they are said to be our best and our brightest. It has been reported that the recent "tax reform bill" will see our current Commander-in-Chief's annual income increased by an estimated $13 million.

Speaking to the endless pillaging and plundering (in and around 1997 to 2001), in his book *Robbing Us Blind*, author Steve Brouwer stated, "The skewing of income statistics was so extreme because those in the top 1% were treating themselves to an enormous windfall of 15%… Referring to the shenanigans of the first Bush administration and the avaricious at the top he concluded: "These thieves have raked in so much that most Americans have gained little or nothing ever since the first Bush Gang appeared on the scene at the beginning of the 1980s."

Although there is a considerable amount of information regarding crime, we would like to wind down this part of the discussion with what was called an "incisive expose of the social and political roots of poverty" by the well-received author Michael Harrington, entitled *The New American Poverty* (1984). Harrington's other publications included *The Other America*, which is said to have impacted President John F. Kennedy so profoundly that it prompted him to take action and address the critical problem of poverty in the country over which he presided.

The New American Poverty points out that "the main victims of the crime wave, it must never be forgotten, are the poor and the minorities." Whenever addressing statistics that show a high rate of crime among blacks, it is also important to note that most of this crime is black on black. At the time of this study it was discovered that black women were the main recipients of the black crimes that were being committed. Within the same paragraph Harrington writes, "Indeed Silberman points out, there is discrimination in the underworld itself:

The professional criminals tend to be whites from working class, or even middle class backgrounds; the 'opportunist' lawbreakers who take a chance when they see one, are by contrast, predominantly from the poor in general and minority poor in particular."

Following this we read a poignant line by Harrington: "It is ironic that the poor as a group are blamed for a violence that they suffer much, much more from than they inflict." One result of the stereotype that ignores this fact is what Christopher Jencks called "statistical prejudice." Some of the "logical" deductions made from the Bell Curve would have us believe that all crime and criminals are caused by low intelligence and a lack of morals, which may be closely connected for them. However, their assessments are sometimes based on selective tests, and language and conclusions that often seem more subjective than scientific. How is an intelligent, higher functioning offender who enjoys more bounty and less punishment, less culpable than a criminal who is impoverished or just less intelligent?

Whatever the statistics may show, the ongoing inferences made by the authors are harmful to honest reform efforts. Current prisons for profits notoriously mistreat and abuse inmates who generally come from past abuse and deprivation, and who in the end, also happen to be human beings. The proof for the negative effects of solitary confinement on prisoners used by prisons for profit is also clear.

It is important here to note that, following the signing of the Community Mental Health Act by President John F. Kennedy, the conservative Reagan administration turned scores of mentally ill out into the streets (*deinstitutionalization*). The monies that were allocated to help some of the most helpless people in the country were given to the states in the form of block grants, which essentially allowed the states to spend those funds however they chose. This resulted in the plethora of money that was then used to build and support prisons for profit, "the jail industrial complex," which warehouses the mentally ill, the powerless and the voiceless, many of whom are black. It seems unnecessary at this point to expound on the devastating effects that a prison has on those with mental illness, and yet this deliberate and heinous behavior was a crime in itself —a crime that has never been rectified. And because they sell shares on the market, the more people incarcerated, the more profit for prisons (unfortunately for the poor).

What has also not been considered in all this, is that a sizable number of these inmates will one day be set free into our communities. After being treated inhumanely, is it an educated guess that they will be more productive, or more destructive members of our society?

Civility and Citizenship

In a much older definition that the authors chose to use, *civility* is defined as "deference or allegiance to the social order befitting a citizen." The newer definition of "courteous behavior or politeness" is ignored by the authors, which allows them to focus on the words *allegiance* and *deference*.

We were unable to actually locate the older definition of the word civility as used by the authors, although we are confident in their researching of the term. When describing civilized people as those "who do not need to be tightly constrained by laws or closely monitored by organs of the state" (p. 254) then we felt the need to proceed with a bit of caution. It seems clear that most civilizations have always found the need to have rules and standards in place in order to maintain a functioning, civil society. Human behavior can become erratic and often unpredictable, regardless of one's level of intelligence. When one group of people in a society perceives themselves as being treated differently than another group, under the same rules, how then is a sense of civility to be maintained? Once asked about what he thought of Western civilization, Gandhi replied, "I think it would be a good idea."

Two words used in the concepts presented here are *allegiance*, which is essentially "loyalty," and *deference*, which is defined as "submission or courteous yielding to the opinion, wishes or judgment of another." Depending on the context in which these terms are used they could be seen as meaning different things. When someone yields to the wishes or opinions of others this isn't necessarily a good thing, especially when they have not consulted their own conscience and what they might really want. Gullible, weak-willed people with low self-esteem are known to be the perfect victims for yielding to cults and trends, and anyone who can *appear* strong and be persuasive. Following this herd-like thinking can also mean having a lack of critical thinking, or having blind faith in someone or something that might not prove to be so beneficial to them in the end.

Again referring to the chapter on crime, the authors manage to associate the growing incivility in America to low cognitive ability. Then, while connecting cognitive ability to voter participation, there may have been a few unseen factors that played into a lack of voter involvement that should have been considered. Voter suppression (supported by the Supreme Court), which has actually been an underhanded practice throughout our country's history, has been overlooked. When people cast their votes, they must now become concerned about their votes even being counted. This has a tendency for some to start distrusting the system and may even discourage them from the voting process entirely. The common refrain is, "What good does it do?" In recent elections we know that voter suppression was rampant and primarily practiced by those who label themselves as conservatives. That these people are allowed to undermine the democratic process is bewildering in itself. The very way in which voters receive their information has been tainted for some time with some media outlets known to disseminate questionable information that has proven to be invalid and inaccurate at times.

The mass media also seems to ignore or circumvent certain facts, that at other times are downplayed or distorted to suit the purposes of those who seek power. We know that the current President actually lost the popular vote by approximately three million votes in the 2016 elections. He then went on to boast about his win and claimed to be a man of the people, although this is not substantiated by his actions or his rhetoric. While we agree with the authors' notion that more consciousness is necessary in these matters, the inferences about voting and civility ring hollow when information is distorted and manipulated, and the peoples' voices are quashed. In this case, those who performed their civic duty were ignored, discouraging voter participation even further. And more Americans have become more convinced of the need to disband the electoral college altogether, which was originally a function of the slave state.

Mudslinging has always been a part of politics, whereby attacks on opponents, whether real or imagined are well documented. However, in modern politics it has turned into a three ring circus. Accusing others of "fake news," some of our politicians attempt to instill fear and anger in order to divide people and secure positions of power. These tactics have been used successfully by tyrants and fascists in the past. In addition, anyone bold enough to speak out and voice another opinion is immediately attacked and accused of somehow being unpatriotic or not concerned about the safety of the country. Demagogues shamelessly blame others for what they themselves do.

Safety and security are the pretense, and violence and mendacity are the means by which tyrants and dictators acquire and maintain power. The most remarkable and regrettable thing about this again, is how the general population could so easily succumb to the ancient ploy of *divide and conquer,* and this should give us all pause. The renowned journalist, Edward R. Murrow once declared that "we must never confuse dissension with disloyalty." Dissent and revolt are at the core of a civil democracy. This country was founded on those very people who in their time, felt the need for an American revolution. And yet, this does not necessitate bloody insurrection, nor does it justify mindless mob violence. So when attempting to establish a direct connection between political participation and intelligence these basic surveys seem to exclude other variables that are never considered in their evaluations.

Intelligence cannot be the only measurement used when we speak about voting and political participation. Some polls show clearly that many people, no matter their level of participation, feel left out of the process. Times change, people change and statistics change. Basic testing with a relatively small amount of people does not provide us with irrefutable proof that I.Q. alone accounts for voter apathy. Political activist, poet and boxing champion Rudolfo Gonzales once called that the two-party system "one monster with two heads that feeds out of the same trough." And as far as voting is concerned, when we are left to choose between the better of two evils, we're still left with evil.

Also in this segment, from what we know about child development, it is difficult to imagine how surveying children's interest in politics could even enter into the discussion. Children around the age of eight or nine years are just beginning to think abstractly. And again, how sample groups are chosen can be critical to statistical outcomes. In fact, in the authors' notes (p. 737), a major study they used, which included 12,000 children, grades 2 thru 8, we find a statement that is a telling example in the phrase, "...although the sample was not strictly representative of the American population." Many American adults can't even identify the three main branches of government. Assessing civility in children could be a tricky endeavor when we consider the changes that they will go through in their lives (and in their brains) and how they may end up. Perhaps civility in children begins with the role models that are set for them at an early age. As mentioned, when parents do not deal with their own issues it can affect the child's ability to learn and develop in a healthy manner. When a child grows up in poverty and deprivation, is it realistic or even fair to place the blame for their later shortcomings on their IQ?

Addressing issues of IQ further, we are also cognizant of the fact that when people need professional services (e.g. from a lawyer to a surgeon), do they seek out someone with experience, or someone who may have gotten higher test scores on their IQ exam? Even if the answer is both, then a deciding factor may still be experience. If I'm putting my life into the hands of an airline pilot, do I prefer an experienced pilot, or a smarter one that's just out of training? Samuel Clemens once exclaimed: "I do not let my schooling get in the way of my education."

We mentioned earlier about the multiple stories of bright and educated business executives who are charged with crimes like fraud, money laundering and tax evasion. These more sophisticated types of crimes likely require more intelligence and planning, and are becoming more and more of a problem. We wonder if these perpetrators could be seen as being more civil because they're smarter. It seems that some people steal out of need and some steal out of greed. One of these groups is considered smarter, and yet which group has been shown to receive more exoneration and leniency in sentencing?

Beyond the obvious monetary gain of this type of criminal is the notion that the ego is seldom satisfied and more is never enough. As mentioned, there is a great deal of fear and insecurity that go along with the insatiable desire to have it all. In a culture that teaches bigger is better and having more is the ideal, should we be surprised at the behavior that we are now witnessing? Is the incivility we see everywhere only found in those who are less intelligent?

If our psychological observations are accurate, then the attempts to fill the empty void inside with things outside ourselves is not very gratifying. It is also apparent that those empty beings who control, exploit and oppress others for their own gain are working against the grain of their own **professed** civil, ethical and moral standards. Maybe this is why so many of these people seem so angry and upset all the time, haunted by their own unconscious, for they have no conscience.

Sometimes it is important to have a more objective view of our own behavior even though it might be a hard pill to swallow. A noted outside observer of American culture, Alexis de Tocqueville once wrote:

"It is odd to watch with what feverish ardor the Americans pursue prosperity, and how they are ever tormented by the shadowy suspicion that they may not have chosen the shortest route to get it… They clutch at everything but hold nothing fast, and so lose grip as they hurry after some new delight." Written in 1839, one could easily conclude that after all this time, nothing has really changed.

So, in attempting to connect civility to intelligence we mustn't forget that along with the privatization of our school systems, cuts in education and the soaring costs of higher education, other relevant factors that impede knowledge and civility must be strongly considered. To add to these problems are the increasing number of schools for profit who advertise themselves as "colleges" or "universities." While some seem legitimate, others are merely diploma mills that are training grounds for fulfilling the needs of corporate America. While these vocational schools market themselves as colleges, they are in actuality trade schools that do not provide a well-rounded education. A number of these organizations have faced serious legal problems for providing questionable training and not following through on the promises that they made (e.g. Trump University). Does a lack of education or a lack of knowledge affect our civility and how we conduct ourselves as citizens?

The Greek paradigm (*paideia*) that was employed in the West was adopted here precisely because it is an effective model of a comprehensive education. It seems as though the current trend is to eliminate the liberal arts and diminish the importance of the social sciences so that a truly well-rounded education is not obtainable. These objectives were made clear in remarks made by the current Secretary of Education, whose obvious goal is to dismantle the education system, and consequently deny the valuable education that our authors propose is so essential. The Secretary has even taken steps to ensure that these fly-by-night "universities" are allowed to operate with impunity. We have also learned that these training mills target those people on the lower end of the socioeconomic ladder. We would ask where the merit and virtue lie in guiding already struggling people to institutions that more often cast unwitting young students into debt, with nothing more than a precarious outcome? We also believe that it would be immensely beneficial to society if more studies were done on the intelligence and behavior of the people who make these vital decisions, prior to putting them into positions of such importance.

With all the emphasis on tests and IQ what is not considered is the power of emotions, which we contend is of equal importance. In our view those who operate primarily from a thinking perspective are often lacking in the area of feelings. While we understand the importance of thinking and reasoning we also believe that at the other end of that spectrum are our human emotions.

The different aspects of our humanity, like civility, may be more difficult to assess by statistical analysis alone. Over many decades of empirical observation, we can surmise that it is difficult to sort out priorities and what is important by thinking alone. Observations in various settings have shown that feelings often serve as an evaluatory function. In a court of law for instance, we've observed what often plays out in a critical jury trial. Once the witnesses testify and the evidence is weighed, a final decision is made, not just by the evidence and information presented, but by human emotions. Any seasoned attorney knows that persuasive closing arguments may well involve eliciting feelings from jurors in order to influence their final decision.

Civility, citizenship, and ethical conduct are not just about what people think, but also how they feel, and data can't show us this. We also believe that people can maintain a facade of civility, while feeling an entirely different way on the inside. And the function of feeling is of paramount importance in attempting to understand our thought processes. We clearly live in a country that overvalues the thinking function and ignores or minimizes the function of feeling. For instance, we don't generally express strong feelings of anguish and grief unless someone or something held great value or importance to us. If our thinking tells us that, to display emotions is a weakness, or that we just shouldn't think about it, this can lead to a psychic dilemma. Thinking provides us with information about the subject or the object, while feelings tell us what it is worth to us; how much we value it.

As corporations get bigger and bigger, with more and more power they seem hard pressed to create balanced, pragmatic solutions that work fairly and effectively for everyone. Some have even suggested that this is not possible. When we use only data and statistics to guide our decisions then the possibilities certainly become more limited and out of reach. At a time when critical thinking combined with an understanding of our feelings is so vital, is it intelligent to dismiss other possibilities? The great intelligence of Einstein shone through in his science, but his profundity was captured when he stated that information was not knowledge. We would like to extend that idea by suggesting that… knowledge is not wisdom.

Middle Class Values

In the conclusion to Part II of the book is a segment in which Herrnstein and Murray relate middle-class values to civility. In their use of a series of *yes and no* questions they attempt to correlate the two. Stressing again that many of us are not researchers, it seems logical to wonder just how values are defined here. What holds a value for one person may carry a different value for another, or for that matter, no value at all. Not surprisingly, the desired outcome here was to provide some evidence that IQ plays the most significant role in establishing who holds the "correct" values and civility, as determined by the authors and these particular surveys.

It seems that people of color are not proportionately represented in this testing either, in fact they don't appear to have been represented at all. We can only assume that people of color also have values. It would also be interesting to know how this Middle-Class Values Index was developed, and exactly how the nature of the questions themselves were developed. It seems that what is vitally important to an individual is difficult to determine with yes and no questions. From the past we have learned that surveys can be structured in a way that facilitates the answers that are beneficial to the interviewer. An old expression has it that, in order to obtain the right answers, you have to ask the right questions. Can the "right" questions be designed to serve the objectives of the examiner? We also know that over the past several decades, both scientists and the general public have become more concerned about the potential ethical problems that can arise in scientific research (Robertson, 1987).

In designing this analytical tool, the researchers tell us that they have excluded those who did not complete high school, those who had never been incarcerated, those who were unwed mothers, and those who were no longer married to their first husbands. In being selective in this survey we notice something peculiar about the excluded groups: "Why are unwed mothers left out of a survey assessing American values?" The other question is: "Why is a woman, no longer married to her first husband, also excluded from this survey?" And how does their exclusion provide us with a more accurate assessment of overall middle class values? One could surmise that being unwed, being a single mother, or not staying married to one's first spouse must have somehow been unacceptable when determining values and civility in middle class society.

It is unfortunate that these people did not meet the stereotypical criteria of a moral citizen. And yet the real intentions of those who were assessing the value of smarter whites as being "more likely to be, and more capable of being made into, a civil citizenry" is never questioned. Currently we are dealing with the indictment of wealthy, intelligent parents in a scandal (referred to as *Varsity Blues*) that is unprecedented in our history and in the world of education. With no regard for honesty or meritocracy, several of America's brighter and wealthy parents have been indicted on charges of bribery, deceit, cheating and other bad behavior, in an effort to have their children admitted to ivy league colleges. This also involved a number of the institutions' staff and personnel. It was also revealed that this was more common than we had thought. So much for our high IQ's, high-minded civility and esteemed middle class values.

Ethnic Differences in Cognitive Ability

"Intellectual fashion has dictated that all differences must be denied…, but nothing in biology says this should be so." (p. 272) It would seem that we're fighting for differences here, rather than trying to find our commonality. And nothing in any of the sciences tells us just to focus on our differences either. It also seems that maybe it's not just "intellectual fashion" that attempts to deny differences, but rather the desire for intelligent, fair-minded people to see people as more equal than different.

From the Bible to the Constitution, the urge to try to see people as equal has always been a challenge. If the proof is in the pudding, then our treatment of one another would suggest that the recipe we are using will require some new and different ingredients. And while the authors have been dismissive of egalitarianism, it would seem to be the most pragmatic and humane path to take. In a generous and well-meaning society, the balance and harmony we seek in our outer world is related to the balance and harmony we find within.

Studies in biology have taught us that all humans are 99% or more the same in our DNA structure. This might suggest that we are far more alike than we are different. And while there are certainly different levels of cognitive ability, many of the differences that we focus on may be of our own choosing. As we peer through our psychological lens we can see that prejudice and racism, for instance, are probably not part of our DNA. Social scientists would suggest that this is learned behavior. Of course concentrating on the differences in others can create fear and animosity in certain types of people, and it is here where we begin to look closer at the age-old phenomenon of *scapegoating*.

So before continuing on in this segment we would like to elaborate on thinking that goes back to the time of the Greeks (*pharmakos/pharmakon*) and was also a distinctive practice of the Hebrews. Maybe a telling question is, with all of our intelligence and cognitive ability, how can this ancient problem still persist in modern societies today? In studies of primitive psychology, we see that the historical phenomenon of scapegoating is found in virtually every civilization, but it is best known as a Judaic ritual. The scapegoat sacrifice described in the Bible was central in the Yom Kippur ritual.

The original purpose of scapegoat mentality was to rid people in the community of disease, suffering or misfortune. These commonly held ceremonies of riddance were performed to magically transfer evil onto plants, animals or other people. The victim or victims were generally chosen from those who were weak, sick or somehow different. The victim would then be driven into the desert or the wilderness where they were left to perish. At times, the victim would be stoned or beaten prior to their exile, just for good measure.

It is of great importance to understand that underlying this outer behavior is a psychological process, an unconscious process which temporarily reduces or eliminates stress and anxiety. In studies of primitive cultures this seems to have provided a release of the perceived evil from the members of the community. However, much like modern day stress and anxiety, if inner issues are not addressed effectively, they only return and the cycle continues. In scapegoating psychology, new victims are then sought out. In various sociological studies these behavior patterns play out over and over again, in families, in communities, in groups and in our national politics. Since in our view this is not an entirely conscious process, then it is all the more important to become more aware. The dire need to understand our own unconscious content and to strive for genuine harmony and balance in the human psyche is more than evident. We contend that the darker chapters of history will continue to be written with the horror stories that reflect our unconscious behavior, unless and until this balance is accomplished.

At this point in our discussion it is interesting to consider why someone would spend so much time and so many resources in an effort to point out the differences and the intellectual inferiority of others. Is this done only for political and economic gain? If we believe in the principle of opposites, then it turns out that we are all a little bit saint and a little bit sinner. We were all gifted with different levels of skills, talent and abilities, and others may have been more or less fortunate in acquiring those gifts.

While we agree that the role of cognitive ability plays an important part in our lives, focusing on intelligence and ethnic differences only plays a role if we allow it to. We also believe that it is important to look at the qualities and traits that make us the same. We may possess individual genes and intelligence that are different from others, but if we lose our sense of fairness, compassion and humanity, and focus on differences, how do we maintain the social cohesion and civility that the authors claim to adhere to?

When taken at face value, blacks and Latinos have higher arrest rates. We have suggested that what is needed are extensive studies on how poverty and racism play a role in their behavior, instead of attacking or discarding whole groups of human beings. This seems like a fair and civil thing to do. The ongoing problem of racism and the treatment of those who are considered less in our society have not been ameliorated by science, and data and statistics have done little to rectify the wrongs done to the less fortunate. In fact, we know that the information provided in tomes like The Bell Curve has had significant influence in ensuring that those lives are never changed in a positive way.

To add to the discussion, and supporting our ideas about crime and criminals, in his book *The Crime of Punishment* (1968), distinguished psychiatrist Dr. Karl Menninger wrote, "Included among the crimes that make up the total are those which we commit, we noncriminals… These are not listed in the statistics… But our crimes make the recorded crimes possible, even necessary; and the worse of it is we do not even know we are guilty." Later, Menninger writes, "I suspect that all the crimes committed by the jailed criminals do not equal in total social damage that of the crimes committed against them."

In a final noteworthy and timely statement from Dr. Menninger we read, "In the last analysis this becomes a question of personal morals and values. No matter how glorified or how piously disguised, vengeance as a human motive must be personally repudiated by each and every one of us. This is the message of old religions and new psychiatries."

We contend that measuring ethnic differences to point out our superiority and give us a social advantage is driven by the darkness within. We will only add that if our intentions are towards a cohesive, peaceful and harmonious world, then the statements and inferences made by the authors in this study do not support those goals. What we have witnessed up to this point is an underlying message of spurious superiority, unwarranted innuendos, divisiveness and a conflictual tone that is both dangerous and self-serving. This mindset should not be taken lightly, because as Dr. King aptly noted, "… the ultimate logic of racism is genocide."

The Demography of Intelligence, and the Perpetuation of Poverty

The next chapter of the book (*The Demography of Intelligence*) immediately begins with the inference that the problems we are facing begin with the less intelligent immigrants that are entering this country, which is also the argument of the current administration. Since the poor and the disadvantaged are the usual targets for scapegoating and mistreatment their exodus would make sense. By the way, the suggestion here is that these invaders become less intelligent as they enter. The fact that it is acceptable and even legal for them to seek asylum here because it is written into our laws does not appear to be an issue for our authors or other sanctimonious patriots.

The next supposition is that these ignorant hordes are actually deteriorating the hereditary quality of Americans themselves. No causal link or valid statistics are provided for these assertions. In fact the authors fail to distinguish between those who are immigrants and those who are refugees, an important distinction. People who attempted to escape hunger, violence, oppression and even death have been welcomed into this country since World War II. In an attempt to assuage our guilt about the refugees who were refused entrance from Nazi Germany, a sincere effort was made to change our laws so that we might live up to the inscription at the base of that famous statue in the New York harbor.

However, this has all since been changed and refugees fleeing violence and oppression are now being thrown into American internment camps by the thousands, with special "kiddie prisons" for children. It puts one to mind of the Japanese internment camps when hard working, law abiding Japanese citizens were ruthlessly thrown into prison camps here during WWII. The only crime of these unfortunate scapegoats was that they sought a better life in a land that's known as freedom. We may have missed something here, but it seems that a vast majority of America's most successful businessmen, politicians and celebrities are either immigrants themselves or descendants of immigrants.

The newer immigration policies, while rejected by most fair-minded Americans, are now being expanded by the current administration. Dr. Scott Allen of Homeland Security has asserted that the problem is that the administration insists on prioritizing confinement over care, creating deplorable conditions for families, and particularly for their innocent children. He has spoken openly about his disdain for the current administration's "willful policy of causing harm to children." When non-profit companies, who set up prison camps were found to be corrupt, lucrative government contracts were then turned over to private, for-profit companies for further exploitation. Callous political decisions and well paid care-less companies are the cause of the death of six refugee children to date.

And yet, we do not hear the usual and proper outrage from the podium or the pulpit. It seems that, even in the face of dying children, the voices of those champions of truth and justice, have grown cold and silent. And with all the talk about the evil in the world, we refuse to see the evil in ourselves. As the learned psychiatrist, Dr. Edward Edinger once observed: "And if you have eyes to see you can see it all around you: human beings have almost no capacity to endure awareness of their own evil. Just a wee little glimpse of the evil aspect of oneself and one is overwhelmed and demoralized."

It is important here to note the precise definition of the term *dysgenics*, used by the authors in this segment. The new American Heritage Dictionary defines this term as "The belief that deterioration of the human gene pool occurs by the increased survival and reproduction of people with undesirable traits." In a later discussion it will become easy to see why the authors of The Bell Curve have chosen to use the term *dysgenics* over the more offensive and better-known term *eugenics*. The authors have stated that they borrowed the dysgenics term from the study of *population biology*, or, *population genetics* and we are unclear about how *dysgenics* or *eugenics* are actually used in population genetics. Of course the word *eugenics* has the definition of "improving the gene pool by encouraging the reproduction of those considered to possess desirable traits, while discouraging the less desirable to mate and produce offspring." It is also interesting to note that in the same paragraph (p. 346) the authors associated "a period of optimism" with Osborn's Eugenic Hypothesis, which was first presented in 1940. The avoidance of the word *eugenics* seems like an attempt to euphemize the term by using the term *dysgenics*. Regardless, both are closely related but it was the term *eugenics* that became so loathsome and unpopular.

We can't be certain about a vague reference to Becker in this part of the text, however we let the following statement speak for itself, "… motherhood imposes greater cost in lost opportunities on a privileged woman than on an unprivileged in the contemporary West." (p. 344) This section may also be one of those places where we would have welcomed an opportunity to view the data that might support these speculative claims.

In this section, to portray a privileged woman of means as somehow disadvantaged defies reason and common sense. This seems to speak more to a biased and opinionated view toward the women who are truly disadvantaged. We are not clear about just what opportunities are lost to women of privilege. In our experiences, women of means can usually afford daycare, maids and nannies more-so, than say a single woman who lives in poverty and requires public assistance. Women of affluence also appear to have the time, means and access to an education that better enables them to "plan their babies carefully." This section suggests that women of lesser means just don't plan, or just don't care about their own offspring. Is it at all possible that poor people struggle in just addressing the day to day needs of survival and caring for their families? Never having had any of these experiences, some people probably aren't able to fathom the struggle for basic survival, where basic needs might take precedence over worrying about whether to choose Gucci or Lauren.

Scratching and clawing for our basic needs is outlined as a first priority in the *hierarchy of needs theory* by noted psychologist, Abraham Maslow. Later concerns for self-actualization are eclipsed by basic survival needs for food and shelter. How do people contemplate becoming a doctor or a professor if they are facing poverty every day? If we follow the authors' line of thinking, then the impoverished are merely dolts who have no concerns whatsoever in doing better or having more. And materialism and having more are what the culture teaches is good and even admirable. They fail to mention in this narrow mindset that not everyone will have the means to purchase whatever they want. Enter predatory lending and the credit industry, otherwise known as indentured servitude, where money-making systems of peonage are set up by our best and our brightest to take advantage of everyone -equally of course.

And as a final display of their disdain for a system that was set up to help the less fortunate, we read that, "for women in the West who live near the poverty line, having a baby is either free or even profitable..." This they say "depends on the specific terms of the welfare system in their country." They may have confused this country with more generous countries that actually show concern for their less privileged citizens. They apparently hadn't noticed the harsh cuts and restrictions surrounding welfare since their conservative campaign took hold, and those programs have been mostly abandoned or underfunded since the war on the poor began.

The visual set up here is that welfare recipients are living high off the hog from meager welfare payments. This is ludicrous and these statements are not supported with the graphs and charts that are usually provided to support some of their other claims. And again, they have failed to address the government's practice of freely doling out our resources to corporations, costing us all a fortune.

Welfare and helpful social programs in this country began with the acknowledgment of low wages, mostly to immigrants at the time. There was also a general awareness of the lack of opportunity for this population. The working poor are not just a small unfortunate group that are found in our past, and the struggle for a living wage continues to be necessary, created by those for whom generosity is lacking and more will never be enough.

The most renowned authority on the history of welfare policy in the United States, Walter I. Trattner, states: "A growing concern with child welfare, however, was not merely a matter of pity or compassion. Indeed, it resulted above all from the fact that most citizens viewed the child as the key to social control. If future generations were to possess the strength of mind, body and character to become good, self-supporting citizens, able to assume the responsibilities and burdens of democratic rule, they had to be protected as children. Youngsters, in other words, are the hope -or the threat- of the future." (*From Poor Law to Welfare State*, 1974)

If safeguarding our children is vital, it then follows that helping and protecting their primary caregivers is also a natural and necessary obligation. In our discussions about unwed mothers, we need to emphasize that there are many males in this society who abdicate their responsibility and are not held accountable. In their statistics, the writers of the Bell Curve seemed to have overlooked a relevant variable: all men who shirk their responsibilities and leave women in financial dire straits. In their view, women's poverty is always the fault of the person who has been victimized by it.

As far back as 1904, Robert Hunter in his classic book *Poverty* proclaimed, "Poverty degrades all men who struggle under its yoke, but the poverty which oppresses children is a monstrous and unnatural thing, for it denies the child growth, development, strength; it robs the child of the present and curses the man of the future." The very fact that this volume was written 115 years ago should clearly say something about the endless struggle for social and economic justice in the land of plenty.

In the present attitude towards the least of our brothers and sisters, any sympathetic or charitable tone has changed dramatically and has been replaced by a cold and callous apathy towards those who are different or who simply have less. During a past era when this same attitude prevailed, President Roosevelt (F.D.R.) fought to provide assistance to the needy in an atmosphere that caused him to accuse his opponents of being "frozen in the ice of their own indifference." Apparently, the multitude of self-professed believers of the kind and loving Nazarene, so beloved by our nation, have forgotten or just disregarded his teachings.

Further into *The Demography of Intelligence* (p. 358) the authors again express anti-immigrant sentiments that have contributed to the harsh policies that continue into the present. The ongoing inference that there is an extreme danger of immigrants and minorities "putting downward pressure on the distribution of intelligence" in our country is neither accurate nor is it scientific. This may also be the pejorative rhetoric that has caused all their diligent efforts to be labeled as eugenic. The reality that we are a nation of immigrants and that this country was built on the backs of immigrants and slaves fails to enter into their discussion. So frightened that they might lose their ill-gotten gains, it appears that some people will use any means necessary to hold on to their wealth with a white-knuckle grip. In the East, controlling others has been likened to grasping a handful of water; the tighter you grip, the less you have.

In their ongoing assault on immigration, the social measures (e.g. welfare and the social safety net) that attempted to ensure some opportunities and more economic parity, are now re-framed to suggest that these humane programs make America an easy target for opportunists. The authors heralded a time when "there were no guarantees, no safety nets." This also perpetuates poverty, cheap labor and harsher immigration laws. After all, it's always been about **them** bringing **us** down, with no discussion about the rampant greed, corruption and malfeasance that have brought us all to the precipice.

In further efforts to instill the notion that they're "taking our jobs" we find, "… immigrants as a whole have more steeply rising earnings than American natives of equal age and measured skills."
The menial jobs taken by most immigrants are precisely the jobs that many Americans refuse to take, and information from other sources has shown that blacks and Latinos have proportionately lesser incomes

than their white counterparts. As far as real natives are concerned, the true American natives have been relegated to abject poverty on reservation land that no one else wanted.

There is an amusing story about a European immigrant that was lured to this nascent country by the promise of prosperity and a better life. He said that he observed three things about the country that encouraged his migration here: He said that upon his arrival, he first noticed that the streets were not paved with gold as he was originally told; the second thing he observed was that the streets were not paved at all, and lastly, it dawned on him that it was **he** that was going to have to pave them.

When referring to Latinos, which we can only assume covers a variety of dark-skinned individuals, we forget that the refugees seeking asylum in the U.S. do not come here by choice, as touched on earlier. The recent refugees have not come from Mexico, but rather through Mexico. A careful examination of the causes for their fleeing has been mentioned, but along with global warming, refugees from Guatemala, Honduras and El Salvador were actually created by American foreign intervention. This includes widespread invasions, the usurpation of existing governments, financial hegemony of weaker countries, along with wars of occupation. Those different groups of unwanted refugees that are fleeing violence, hunger and oppression were actually created by us. Their reward for seeking freedom and asylum has been the criminalization of their desperate acts and their imprisonment. An old Somali saying has it that "Nobody leaves home, unless home is the mouth of a shark."

Moreover, the Mexican people themselves owned at least eight states in the West and Southwest which were taken as the result of yet another invasion. Following the Mexican-American War, the great American general and President, Ulysses S. Grant proclaimed that America should never again invade a third world country and do what it had done in Mexico. Of course, a sense of entitlement and exceptionalism prevent any further discussion of the matter and our southern neighbors, much like the American Indians remain, in the words of Professor David J. Weber, "foreigners in their native land."

We discussed earlier the newer class of citizens known as the "working poor." Sometimes working as many as two or three jobs, the reward for these hard-working Americans has been only higher costs at the marketplace and the gas pumps, fewer rights and benefits for workers, privatization, and jobs that do not provide living wages. At this pace, it has been suggested that America is quickly becoming a third world country itself. While the wealthy reap the benefits of a selective corporate government we are learning more and more each day about the disparity that has been anything but accidental. Some forty years ago the Wall Street Journal printed: "Statistical evidence already suggests that the American Dream is fading." (March 31, 1981)

As Leonard Beegley points out it in *The Undeserving Poor*, "Researchers believed that statistics could measure poverty objectively. In fact, because poverty defies scientific measurement, all measures reflect political judgments." (Katz, 1989) Other concerned authors and scholars have chimed in on the growing poverty and disparity that has always been ignored and dismissed by those cognitive elitists who have just been more intelligent and ambitious. Noted author and activist, Michael Harrington, while speaking to institutionalized poverty wrote, "There is something much worse: a deep structural source of a new poverty that could persist into the indefinite future." Written thirty-five years ago, Harrington's eerie prediction has come to pass. He theorized that poverty and inequality, though equally related, are not the same thing. The point is made, because he says, "… it is crucial in dealing with one of the conservative critiques of the very idea of an antipoverty effort."

Harrington points to the conservative mindset of then Senator, Barry Goldwater in the sixties who claimed that poor people were just a statistical fact, and that it was a mathematical impossibility to abolish poverty; that there will always be inequality. This is the thinking and these are the pronouncements of higher intellects that in one fail sweep relegated the poor to eternal damnation.

It is also important to note that this is a long-held tenet and an argument of some religious conservatives, who have leaned so far right that they are wrong, and still wreaking havoc. Harrington then goes on to state unequivocally that perpetual poverty is a fabrication that is "simply not true." (*The New American Poverty*, 1984) We would like to provide the reader with just two more examples of the inequities in our society, and how they compare with other parts of the world.

Briefly, along with so many others, we hold a great deal of respect and admiration for the diligent efforts of the late Michael Harrington, and his dedication and commitment to what he referred to as, "the pilgrimage toward our humanity."

Citing as an example the "lowest fifth," as those at the bottom of the ladder are referred to in this country, the author states that the lowest fifth exists in Sweden as well. But, he states, that in both absolute and relative terms this population is better off than the lowest fifth in the U.S. "It is less poor." It also has a lower infant mortality rate, another vital area where we lag behind (statistics at the time in the 80's, showed a 16.1% rate in the U.S. vs. 8.6% in Sweden; and with 13% of Americans under the poverty line vs. 3.5% of Swedes). This translates into the people who are at the bottom fifth in the U.S. being much poorer than those of the lowest fifth in Sweden. We also know that the infant mortality rates for blacks in America are three times higher than that for Swedes as a whole.

To add another interesting tidbit, Americans spend more than most countries combined on healthcare and yet we are ranked 34th in the world for our overall health. Our burning question is: Just where do our interests lie? It seems clear that consciously or unconsciously, people spend their time and resources on what they value most. What isn't clear, is why we spend so much more on so much less.

Turning to just one more relevant example, we find that the income of the top quintile in the U.S. was more than eight times that of the bottom quintile, but that gap has widened. The author then goes on to write that in Japan, the difference was five to one. He also keenly points out that Japan "is hardly an egalitarian society." In ending our Japanese example Harrington states, "The American poor are thus more 'unequal' than the Japanese poor." So, plainly put, America continues to fall far behind ten or more advanced nations in terms of its per capita wealth. Consequently, the lowest fifth in our country receive a smaller percentage of a smaller economic pie than do the lower fifth in the European welfare states.

"Goldwater's attempt to make a statistical case for that biblical statement so often quoted on the right -that the poor will always be with us, a holy witness to eternal truth- fails" (Harrington, 1984). To frame poverty and deprivation as caused by lower intelligence, personal failure or moral weakness is in itself morally reprehensible, and it is unacceptable. Along with his father, an early and great political and religious influence, Cotton Mather (1663-1728) exclaimed, "For those who indulge themselves in idleness, the express command of God unto us is, that we should let them starve." Apparently, Rev. Mather couldn't have considered that American jobs might be shipped overseas, or that those who actually worked for a living would not be payed a living wage. And he may have missed the biblical passage about loving thy neighbor as thyself, or Jesus' own crusade to help the poor and needy.

We would like to end this segment with one more example of the fact that the problem of poverty and a lack of opportunity have been manufactured and perpetuated by those who suffer from a sclerosis of the spirit, and not by those who bring it on to themselves. In 1969 Edith Green on the House, Education and Labor Committee observed that, "… probably our most enduring monument to the problem of poverty has been the creation of a poverty industry" (*Politics of the Rich and Poor*, Phillips, 1990).

For some, creating a society that provides opportunities to become a productive member of society seems like a reasonable, intelligent course of action. Some might even determine that it is in the best interest of our communities and our economy. But from what we've learned, our psychological projections never seem to make reasonable or logical sense. Especially at this point in our history, we can subscribe to the archaic and misguided notions of the past, or we can open our hearts and our minds to help those who struggle for their daily bread in the present. We can also do nothing, which is also a choice.

Affirmative Action in Higher Education

Looking at this chapter we again find some assertions that seem more subjective than factual. Having already spoken briefly about education, we again find the authors ignoring reality and the plight of the vulnerable. Herrnstein and Murray remark that when white students look around on college campuses, "they see blacks and Latinos doing poorly in school." We can only hope that these brighter, whiter students also see the human beings that are their fellow students. This comment is then followed by another unfounded accusation, when the authors proclaim that the disparity between blacks and whites was the probable explanation for an increasing animosity and high dropout rates "that have troubled American campuses."

It is relieving to discover that the dropout rates were caused by minorities' bad academic performance and not actual racial differences. The only "animosity" that we've heard about recently is with the system itself. Other than drunkenness, debauchery, and your everyday cheating, we were unable to locate data that showed (current) significant racial problems on "troubled American campuses." And any violence in today's schools, has been encouraged by the political elites who have lobbied for guns on school campuses. It is also interesting to learn that concerned white students, who were intellectually superior, would have shown any concern or alarm about their inferiors doing poorly in school. After all, by the authors' own account, wasn't their failure just to be expected?

The dictionary defines *Affirmative Action* as "A policy or program that seeks to redress past discrimination through active measures to ensure equality, as in education or employment," By all indications, the end results have not been achieved. Attempts at rectifying the maltreatment and abuse of minorities by the system also infers that some people, at least at the time, may have had a conscience. Concerned about imaginary losses, many Americans now choose to allege *reverse discrimination*. In the volume that we are reviewing we find the untenable argument that by helping the disadvantaged, people of wealth and privilege are treated unfairly. Disallowing an education to poorer members of our society also ensures that minorities will continue doing the menial labor, and provide scapegoats for business and the wealthy for years to come. With the advent of robots and artificial intelligence maybe the proponents of oppression will now be able to choose the color, intelligence and disposition levels of their servants and handmaids. Determined, dysphoric elitists are now working overtime to ensure that disinformation and inequality prevail on all college campuses.

Throughout the text we are reviewing we find feeble attempts at a concern for fairness, and we can also detect some measure of favoritism toward the Asian population, who have managed to escape the disparaging comments made towards other people of color. Even though the Asian population makes up a smaller portion of the overall population, we know that they too have suffered discrimination and bigotry, as is well documented. We are of the opinion that **no** minority or person of color should be discriminated against or mistreated in a country that extols freedom, justice and equality as its highest virtues. Perhaps our actual practices should meet our espoused principles.

We are reminded especially of the attempted genocide of the American Indians (a term preferred over "American natives," by Russell Means of the American Indian Movement). Anyone born in the U.S. can lay claim to being an American native. As mentioned earlier, Mexicans owned land in this country two hundred years before the Europeans crossed the Appalachians. We are also painfully aware of the horrors of slavery and the blacks who were introduced to this country in slave ships, many perishing from the journey alone. These groups have all been exploited in order to create wealth for European invaders. And maybe now we can begin an honest discussion about fairness and equality.

In Chapter 19, authors of the Bell Curve even go so far as to reject decisions that were made by the Supreme Court and other legislators at the time. Disingenuous remarks made about trying to eliminate racism and racial differences are also unrealistic, as long as individuals are unaware of their own behavior and their own darkness. While some theories posit that racism is a learned behavior, we believe that it also comes from a deeper, darker place inside of us. We also know that when children are treated with love and respect, and modeled healthy behavior, then they are **more likely** to be more loving and respecting adults. And while they live what they learn, children can also be driven by other inner factors. Under the right circumstances, most people are capable of anything.

The merging of learned behavior with unconscious projection can quickly become a recipe for disaster. When by culture or family we learn that bad behavior is acceptable, as in today's sociopolitical climate, then we have tapped into a wellspring of darkness that can only be kept in check when it is first acknowledged, and then, when it is dealt with in an effective manner, which requires self-awareness, self-honesty and our own diligent *inner* work. If this were such an easy thing to do, then maybe more people would be doing it. In a just and civilized society, social parity would also mean fair laws that apply to everyone equally, along with social **and** economic equality.

The authors correctly suggest that Affirmative Action has not succeeded in elevating those that it targeted. While more current research is in order, it appears that much in line with protecting their assets, those at the top of the food chain have learned that people who are educated can pose a threat to the status quo. These common sense ideas have no need for statistical support and are well understood by the general public. The negative words and actions of the current President and his cabinet speak for themselves when it comes to not facilitating freedom and providing equal opportunity.

For those believing in a judgment day, one can only stand by curiously and wonder what rationalizations will be presented at the Pearly Gates. Perhaps they could say that "the devil made them do it." The power to deny others an opportunity to advance, or to even support themselves and live with dignity must be examined closely. It's clear that there is plenty of money in this country, it's just concentrated in too few hands. Never learning the wisdom of the need to fill ourselves up with ourselves, instead leads to narcissism, megalomania, avarice and other forms of ego inflation.

The term *narcissism* itself is yet another concept that is often misused and misunderstood in mainstream America. Without going into too much detail, in our society a narcissist is often misperceived as someone who has too much love for themselves. And while it can look that way, contrary to this understanding, narcissism is not actually about self-love and self-admiration, it is rather about self-loathing. Along with this core notion is the narcissist's feelings of inauthenticity and inner emptiness, and their inability to truly connect with others. The outer facade of bravado and self-assurance often masks an inner core of insecurity and self-doubt.

In his classic bestseller, *The Culture of Narcissism (1979)*, Christopher Lasch elaborated on the dramatic rise and treatment of narcissism in America. He accurately pointed to the primary causes as a materialistic culture, combined with mass consumption and media indoctrination. This disorder has a far-reaching impact on every aspect of our society and we have seen few signs of it subsiding.

Lasch has been critical about the tendency of others to label narcissism as "a metaphor of the human condition." It is important to note that this destructive behavior is not a passing state of mind, and it is not just a normal condition of the species. Lasch refers to this modern character disorder as a form of "psychiatric pathology," which is a devastating and deep-seated illness created by an entire culture of materialism and egocentricity (ego inflation). With an "every man for himself" attitude, egocentrism, and the antiquated notion of rugged individualism as our anthem, nothing could keep us further from cohesion, or even a sense of unity.

The psychological practice of individuation, turning inward and knowing ourselves is not in itself narcissistic, because it is only in coming into balance and knowing who we really are that we are better able to interact in a non-selfish way and have compassion for our fellow travelers. When this is not accomplished then we are endlessly and futilely trying to find outer solutions to inner problems.

Favoring the Fortunate

In a subsection of Chapter 19 (p. 460) the authors provide us with a scenario that depicts a crown prince attempting to gain entrance to Princeton University. This, we assume, is the odd example they use to advance their arguments against Affirmative Action. The authors describe the individual as being a white prince of "pedestrian intelligence," as well as possessing an "indifferent character." So essentially we are presented with an advantaged, apathetic white male of ordinary intelligence. The question then posed by the authors is: "Should Princeton admit the crown prince in preference to the more bright and virtuous students who apply for admissions in droves?" Our first observation is that obviously, each prospective student should be admitted on his or her own merits, their aptitude and their performance. And exactly how virtue is actually used as a standard of measure for entrance into a college is not explained.

This scenario attempts to frame how we might see this and similar issues, and how our esteemed authors would admit the crown prince to Princeton University (old PU), in spite of his average intellect and his indifference. This seems like a strikingly contradictory choice, following the strong arguments against equality for blacks in the previous text. In fact, previously we had been convinced that an average student of lower cognitive ability should not be given an edge in his pursuit to better himself. We assume that women should not be given this opportunity either, particularly single mothers. In any event, a careful read of the earlier text might indicate that now, yes, of course the low-achieving person of royal lineage should have the advantage over others who might be more intelligent -he's white and wealthy.

The reason given for the authors' decision is just how much influence and power his highness would possibly exert over his many subjects. However, it is just as likely that he could turn out to be a tyrant or a scoundrel, which seems to be the global crisis that we are witnessing today. We concur with the old and proven saying that power corrupts and that absolute power corrupts absolutely. The global flight of refugees due to violence, oppression and starvation would paint a slightly darker picture of reality than the authors would have us see when it comes to educated leaders.

The presupposed and triumphant contributions that Harvard, Yale, Princeton or any other ivy league school "would make to human happiness" have not seemed to have fully materialized. The real-life contributions that have been made by these cognitive elites is unclear.

We will not elaborate on the long list of graduates that have used their knowledge and education for things that were more self-serving and less philanthropic. In fact, ivy league schools are notoriously known as the connecting points for the elite businessmen, bureaucrats and politicians of the future.

The final and lofty assumption about Princeton and what it is supposed to render, is that it has now given the apathetic prince the opportunity to "develop into a thoughtful and human adult," as a result of being selected over much brighter prospects who -in the authors' own view- were more qualified and more concerned about their world. The framing of the situation here is important, as we already know that these students started out as human adults, but this does not translate into them becoming more **humane** and sensitive adults. We're hearing from the authors that ivy league schools now have the ability to teach their students how to become more caring and concerned, and this **is** quite a feat. Strolling down the halls of an academic institution I once noticed a very humbling sign in an obscure corner that simply read, "Higher education is just incompetence by degrees."

The story then transforms into a more racially motivated decision involving Princeton's rare choice between a white affluent candidate and a black affluent candidate. The white student here is portrayed as having "more glowing references and higher test scores" than his unfortunate black counterpart. After establishing that both candidates aspire to be attorneys, the authors propose that, "In some sense, the white candidate 'deserves' admission more." Did his test scores and references hint at this? The situation is then framed as, "…who is going to provide more social 'value-added' -adding one more white attorney to the ranks of prominent attorneys, or adding one more black one?" Upon first reviewing these comments, besides being taken aback, we again noticed the confusing assertions that seem to be losing any scientific credibility.

Had the assets of these candidates been reversed, would the white candidate still have been favored by these authors? In this situation, while having higher test scores is certainly a consideration, we have also considered that the color of their skin might be irrelevant in assessing which candidate might actually provide more social value. Looking at the examples of today's politicians and business leaders, it becomes quite clear that one can be white, advantaged and educated and still not make fair, prudent decisions based on what is vital to all the members of our society and our world.

We are not aware of Princeton's actual requirements for admission, and the authors' subjective opinions about the school's objective criteria seem to complicate the matter at hand. The logic the authors give for Princeton's decision-making process is based on the idea that only by expanding the **size** of the next generation of minority attorneys, doctors etc. can society attain racial equality at higher socioeconomic and professional levels. This seems to infer that the school's weakness (Affirmative Action) is to admit students to maintain quotas. However, their reasoning for college admissions is constantly clouded by their language and arguments like "social utility" and "just desserts," their own framework for how helping the disadvantaged is unfair to already-advantaged whites.

They then turn to their trusted data that indicates lower cognitive ability for blacks, never considering the generations of poverty and oppression that have played into a lack of education and opportunity for some less privileged groups. Then, after having confirmed that blacks and minorities have lower cognitive ability on the previous pages, we read (p. 477): "To what extent is society fair when people of similar ability and background are treated as differently as they are now?" Blacks don't often come from similar backgrounds as whites, and the authors would have them treated differently if even they did display similar abilities, which is their main objective here. Let's just look at history and the facts to determine who has actually been treated differently in this country. With all that we've read so far, maybe Princeton should offer a course on *convoluted logic*.

It seems obvious that an attempt at balance in all things, including ourselves, is always a safe bet. It's also obvious that trying to level the playing field by making sure that all Americans have equal access to education is not the egregious crime that some would have us believe.

Furthermore, conflating the discrimination of the black's problems in our society with discrimination of the Jews, while giving their usual nod to Asians, seems a bit confusing, but then racism and bigotry have been known to be selective in their targeting. And we know that all people of color have experienced mistreatment or discrimination in some form or another in this great land of ours. As was suggested before, maybe it's time for a much-needed cultural paradigm shift.

Contrary to conventional wisdom, real happiness does not come from outside ourselves. It does not come from fortune or fame. It is only temporarily found in a new car, a better job or a bigger house. It cannot be obtained by just having an ivy league education or an attractive partner, although knowledge can be helpful. The happiness that is found outside of ourselves is fleeting, and it's clear that no one can be happy all the time. In reality, we are never responsible for the happiness of others and they are never responsible for ours. Our words and actions can be helpful in supporting the lives of others, but we cannot control what they're feeling inside. Attempting to **deny** others of happiness and opportunity appears to be the problem at hand.

So in trying to process all this, we have to understand the power of those who are considered as knowledgeable and educated authority figures. Those considered as experts may possess an intellectual advantage, but how is it being used? Educators and experts who wield a great deal of influence over others and their thinking, also have a great responsibility to be sensitive, ethical, fair and honest, or not.

Aligned with this way of thinking, former President of Harvard University, Drew Faust in a recent public interview, spoke out about her strong desire for inclusiveness at Harvard. When asked about admittance to the school based solely on SAT scores, she asserted that this approach "would be disastrous." She went on to explain that mere test scores reduce individuals to numbers and data.

She clearly understands that measuring people by tests scores alone ignores their individuality, thereby ignoring their humanity. Some would have us believe that the text we are reviewing is innocuous. Some believe that it is poisonous pedagogy. Should anyone decide to read the book in question, we would only ask that readers see beyond the deluge of graphs and charts into what is not clearly being stated, and trust their own judgment, using their heads **and** their hearts.

Affirmative Action in the Workplace

It becomes easier and easier to see the pattern set by the authors and this continues on into the next chapter, *Affirmative Action in the Workplace*. In this chapter the authors allege that police departments across the country are deteriorating and the reason given for this is that the testing is designed to favor minority applicants, and though no evidence is provided for these arguments -possibly due to their scholarship- readers are expected to take these statements at face value. And this unfairness to white officers, the authors say, has been caused by the poor performance of all those inferior minority officers on the streets. So incompetent are these law enforcement officers that even the standard paperwork required in the course of their work negatively affected their performance, as well as destroying their entire department. With no other substantiation of this behavior, the authors point to one article entitled, *A Journalist's Account of the Washington D.C. Police Force.*

It is interesting to note that the journalist who authored this article, and who was chosen to support their theory, was the right-wing reporter Tucker Carlson, who works for conservative media outlets that also serve as the propaganda machine for our current White House. His biased positions are made less credible by his public denigration of minorities and third world countries. He is also notorious for openly chastising and demeaning women. The pejorative comments made about D.C.'s finest also carry over into general statements about "people in the academy," their illiteracy, incompetence, etc. Who "they" really are is not always made clear, however with "their" track record, we can assume that they again are the people of color who risk their lives for their communities, and happen to be black or brown in color.

Using only one other obscure account from a police department in Florida, a blanket statement is made about the deterioration of all departments in the country. We are all aware of the rampant misbehavior and wrongdoing of professionals and nonprofessionals throughout the country. An intelligent suggestion that was overlooked is, when dealing with law enforcement it is important to create outside citizen review boards (which are now allowed by a few departments). Due to the stress and the sometimes violent nature of the job, it is also important to conduct in-depth psychological testing on a regular basis for those officers who operate on the streets. Active and ongoing involvement with the community, its leaders and various local agencies also seems like a prudent thing to do. We would hope that in a corporate culture that teaches all of its citizens to be self-serving and materialistic, that others might see that harmful behavior is not just reserved for law enforcement agencies.

More importantly, we are trying to ascertain precisely what the causal link is between poor police performance and the alleged biased testing in the hiring process. If the inference here is that all this incompetence is solely due to biased, low standards of testing then why not help develop new standards of measurement that do not choose candidates based on the color of their skin. It would also have been more fair to have heard from the accused departments and officers themselves about these serious allegations. We wonder why a concerned journalist would not have cared to interview those in such positions of trust in our society more extensively.

The title of the chart on page 497 speaks volumes, as it relates to other Affirmative Action complaints from the authors: *Job Performance of Black Affirmative Action Plumbers and Pipefitters Compared to White Regular Hirees*. While this could appear to be a benign scientific comparison, a more critical observation would have us ask why the work of black plumbers versus white plumbers would be of such concern that a special chart with statistics had to be created by researchers? It is important to note that the blacks who participated in this study were court ordered employees. Could the fact that this was not their chosen employment, or that they were mandated to do the work, have anything to do with their time and performance on the job? It is also obvious that their *job performance* should not be based only on how long they lasted on the job, but on their actual performance on the job. Also, the authors minimized the study's creator (Silberg) when he posed the possibility that the differences themselves might be the result of bias among the supervisors and the dispatchers.

Not only do we wonder just what proportion of blacks versus whites was used in this study, but how different the outcome might have been by removing court ordered offenders from the equation altogether. Might this be yet another affront to Affirmative Action and the people that these studies feign to do right by? This research seems to appeal to those who require only the slightest excuse for their intransigent positions and their vindictive behavior -we see what we choose to see.

There are ample studies to support the theory that people with certain types of personalities are drawn to certain occupations. In the scenario involving law enforcement (and politics) it is known that these particular positions allow a person to have an element of power and control over others. Combined with the unknown forces within, that we've already alluded to, this can manifest in certain individuals in a way that does not always conform to ethical or appropriate behavior. The deeper need to have power over others and be respected in an authoritarian type, can quickly develop into a dangerous situation when that person perceives a threat or believes that they are being disrespected.

The more extreme cases where citizens are abused or mistreated are tangible examples of the abuse of power, and again, this behavior is dramatically increasing in our society. In recent years there have been several documented cases in which mostly black males have been gunned down by the police, and the victim was later discovered to have been unarmed or nonthreatening. It is also clear that most of these killings were committed by white policemen. We know that these violent acts are often minimized and even condoned, as the perpetrators continue to operate with impunity for their crimes. And yet, we constantly proclaim that **no one** is above the law.

There have also been random studies that indicate that there is a significant amount of domestic violence and spousal abuse that occur within the ranks of the military and law enforcement. While there are certainly law enforcement officials who are upstanding and law abiding, power in the wrong hands can have lethal consequences.

With the amount of stress and responsibility involved in these positions, the possibilities are not hard to imagine. In addition, it is also clear that draconian laws and harsher methods have been proven to be ineffective when dealing with crime and criminals. In the end, an effective and fair way to address crime might mean that, in addition to some form of reasonable punishment, commensurate to the crime, we treat people like human beings. An effective deterrent might be to reduce racial injustice and poverty.

In 1977, social psychologist Phillip Zimbardo conducted a well-known experiment at Stanford University. What turned into a frightening situation began as a research experiment about the roles we play in society, which of course are a part of the socialization process itself. In a simulated prison environment, the students who participated were divided into two groups, the guards and the prisoners. After a period of time something very interesting began to happen. The students who had acted as guards became cruel, so cruel that some students acting as prisoners experienced severe emotional reactions that ranged from anxiety to extreme anger; the kind of anger that is often seen in real penal institutions. So caught up in the roles they were playing, their disturbing behavior caused the experiment to be halted prematurely.

While more research needs to be done in this area, might this study suggest that there are those, who when put into positions of power, might develop cruel and autocratic tendencies? This could also suggest that those people who could already have a propensity for control and dominance, should be tested, screened and background checked prior to being given certain positions of power and authority. And while history and psychology would support these ideas, there have also been a few people in positions of power who become fair and caring leaders, however, they seem to be the exception and not the rule.

When we consider the idea of preexisting patterns in the human psyche (psychological archetypes), this might give us a better understanding of why some people seem to be a natural fit for some positions. We know that problems can arise when we identify with our persona. And from the work of psychologists like Jung, we also know that there are differing psychological types, and this can be quite helpful in understanding behavior. After all, we are not the roles we play, and maybe it is high time for all of us in this culture to find out who we are -who we **really** are!

There are many factors that play into behavior and human interaction in the workplace and at home, and we see people behaving badly everywhere. However, these purported examples of unfairness, that would exclude certain groups from the benefit of fair hiring practices and equality in the workplace, or from a job at all, sound less like scientific research that would benefit employers and employees, and more like ideological separatism.

As we're starting to detect in this section on Affirmative Action, some are compelled to go through great lengths to obtain power, and even more treacherous means to hold on to it. Wouldn't investigating our darker behavior be a more effective strategy in trying to understand peoples' actions and man's inhumanity to man? Maybe a better understanding of our deeper selves should take precedence over judging others by their IQ scores. Only a meaningful change in ourselves can lead us to a new chapter in our new millennium. It seems inevitable that when people look back, they will be disheartened by how our best thinkers did not thoroughly scrutinize those to whom they willingly surrendered so much trust and responsibility.

Moving on in the chapter we are again confronted with ongoing attempts to convince people that hiring practices based on Affirmative

Action create poor productivity and job performance, particularly
when it comes to hiring less intelligent black workers. Using our
common sense and what we know about corporate America today, we
would suggest that this complaint lost its punch long ago. We are all
familiar with the stories of people losing their jobs for a variety of
reasons. More and more we hear that in some of these cases workers
are terminated for invalid reasons or for no reason at all. And we
would be hard-pressed to find documentation kept by corporations that
would openly admit to racial discrimination as a reason for terminating
a worker. In fact, we contend that this is the unchecked behavior that
deteriorates fair labor practices and fairness to all workers.

As far as job performance itself is concerned, there have been recent
law suits that depict how the HR departments in various organizations
have acted as nothing more than the minions of their employers,
embellishing and exaggerating information in an effort to be rid of
certain employees. Firing workers for everything from personal
politics to sexual orientation, employees are not only losing their
benefits, but their rights in the workplace. Even their right to privacy is
now in jeopardy by companies who feel ownership over their
employees. And as mentioned, this callous behavior on the part of
corporate America overtly begins with determined conservatives, who
have targeted the only organizations that would have protected the
rights, wages and benefits of workers.

To be clear, it is not as suggested by the authors, that Affirmative
Action has "imposed second-class citizenship on minorities." It is the
policy-making decisions of those who have no interest in fairness and
equality that keep minorities in their place. Any real understanding of
its historical roots might prove that racism, hatred, war and misogyny
will not be leaving us any time soon, although divisive techniques
could be replaced by more fair and inclusive methods if leaders had
the political will. When a different perspective that includes unity,
cohesion and the common good is adopted, then programs like
Affirmative Action might not be necessary. It is through science that
we've learned that we are more alike than we are different. Our
coming together may even mean our very survival. In keeping with
this philosophy, Eleanor Roosevelt remarked that, "We all must face
the fact that either all of us are going to die together, or we are going to
learn to live together…"

Since so much time and effort have been devoted to the destruction
of Affirmative Action in this volume, we find it fitting to wind down
with a few more bewildering remarks. We read a curious statement on

page 499: "It may be efficient to hire fewer clerks who will be discriminated against but it is not fair." There is first the looming question of how these authors define their sense of fairness, and, unfair to whom? By hiring fewer clerks in this scenario, this can only mean that hiring fewer white clerks would be unfair. This seemingly harmless statement also presupposes that some or all customers who enter these establishments are prejudiced and that people of color "will be discriminated against." So their veiled opinion is that prejudicial behavior towards a clerk of color is inevitable. The efficiency of the business does not seem to be the authors' primary objective here.

We also know that many bigoted people often conceal their prejudicial attitudes in public. We wouldn't want to be **seen** as some kind of racist. So, given a moment to think about it, what then would be their reason for not hiring minorities or people of color? In an underhanded way, the authors seem to be saying that it is not fair to hire fewer whites over minorities so that discrimination would less likely occur. In reality, why would any employer hire less whites in some imagined scenario of future discrimination in his or her business?

It seems clear that people of all cultures and colors work in a variety of businesses and professions, and the business world hasn't collapsed as a part of their being hired, or because of fair hiring practices. To assert that it is somehow harmful for an employer to hire a person of color because a customer might be a racist is misleading. And again, isn't the person who is being turned away for being a minority actually the one who is being treated unfairly? After all, in our society, white people aren't usually refused employment because they're white. This tangled rationale throughout the authors' discussion can only be seen as attempting to influence thought, with underlying intentions of impacting laws and policies as well. And some twenty-five years later, it appears to have accomplished what it set out to do. What does this say about the thinking and attitudes of those who bought into it?

In the final sentence of the same paragraph we read: "Many people would be willing again, to lose some efficiency in return for greater equality." This statement suggests that employers lose efficiency in their business just by having minority workers in the first place. It then suggests that those same employers might prefer that trade-off for greater equality in the workplace. This is contradictory, since in the profit-driven business world, bottom-line thinking would make it difficult to find any corporation that would be willing to sacrifice its productivity and profits in a purposeful effort to create equality among its workers.

Continuing with similar arguments, a more revealing statement appears: "By the standard of proportional equality, there are too many black players in the National Basketball Association compared to the number of white players." This is then followed by the clincher, "No one thinks this is unjust." This example reveals a deeper concern for more than just IQ scores and cognitive ability. We wonder if the authors considered what the NBA and the popular sport of basketball would be like without these talented athletes. They may have also ignored the fact that black players are just better athletes in some sports than white players. This has less to do with the need to focus on balanced numbers in the NBA, and more to do with the authors' obsessions about race and color. Do the large audiences drawn to basketball games also believe that there are too many blacks and not enough whites in the sport, or is it more about the game for them? Ask yourselves if these examples effectively support the authors' fervent arguments to diminish and eliminate Affirmative Action, which was already limited in its success.

And finally, with unabashed relief, we move towards the end of this segment of the book. Throughout this portion of the Bell Curve the writers have assumed that employers are not using standard hiring practices. They have unconvincingly assured us that a clear advantage is given to minorities in all areas of employment, and we assume in sports as well. We continue to wonder who these ideas are intended to help. Employers are under no obligation to provide valid reasons for who they hire or who they fire. The concern now is whether employers hire their workers on the basis of their skills and abilities, or on the basis of their color -we'll never really know. If it's the latter, then we wager that they will miss out on some capable and talented additions to their roster of employees. And the intelligence of these prospective hires that was so important in other areas, has taken a back seat. The irony is palpable: If employees were truly fair-minded and honest, what would be the need for Affirmative Action to begin with?

Moving to a global society finds us all in need of global cooperation, which should probably begin at home. A concerted effort will be essential in dealing with the critical issues of global warming, nuclear self-destruction and diminishing resources. The "us and them" thinking of the past will no longer sustain us because like it or not, we're are all in the soup together.

Power

As Zeus said to Prometheus: *Now you've stolen fire but without justice and reverence, you will lose that very thing that you thought was everything.*

From a psychological perspective, the incessant desire for power and control clearly appears to be over-compensation for fear and insecurity. We also know that power and security are priorities of the human ego.

In considering the mindset of those who seek power, we must return to our childhood experiences. Psychologists have discovered that children who suffer the insufficiencies of childhood and their environment often develop a diminished sense of self-worth and then addictively pursue reassurance and affirmation from others. This can also involve them carrying a great deal of fear and rage, whether they're aware it or not. In fact, beneath all the bluster and bravado fears and insecurities are always lurking.

Consider this country's newly installed leader, who cannot tolerate criticism whether it is negative or constructive. The constant, sophomoric need to make pejorative comments and denigrate others on social media is accompanied by a pitiful cry to be loved and admired by all. His fragile ego, animosity and insecurities govern his psyche. He remains stuck in an infantile mindset, rejecting the very things he needs most. In being self-alienated and not knowing himself, he appears to be oblivious to his own offensive and negative behavior, both online and off, and this speaks to his own avoidance and denial. Sometimes the hardest thing to see is ourselves. We've known for a while now that denial and avoidance are powerful psychological defense mechanisms.

And we mustn't forget that victims of the patriarchy only know how to measure their worth by how much power and money they have. Then, for whatever reason, if they lose their power and possessions -what are they- nothing? It is my firm belief that when future observers of history look back to this era, they will be amazed and bewildered as to why thorough psychological testing was not required of those who were allowed so much power over so many. The renowned philosopher, Nietzsche once, almost inadvertently, described the dispassionate, elitist attitude towards those who are viewed as inferior. He suggested that the general population (the rest of us) are seen as the botched, the bungled, "the expendable masses." Moreover, at the

Constitutional Convention in 1787, a key figure in framing the Constitution, James Madison, set the tone when he stated that the entire political system should be designed "to protect the minority of the opulent from the majority." This, he stated, was the purpose of government. These elitist ideations have never wavered.

And if we have the eyes to see, from the stacking of the Supreme Court and our federal courts, to a total disregard for the Constitution or the rule of law, the execution of unarmed citizens, and the current dismantling of our democracy, the wealthy elitists who don't pay taxes, and are allowed an inordinate amount of power, have run out of patience. They now appear to want it all, and at any cost, as long as it is someone else who pays for it. At the center of all the colluding and chicanery lie the puppeteers, The American Heritage Foundation, whose lust for power and wealth has earned them the title of the "vicious avaricious," and whose only concerns are about power, riches and status.

Nietzsche also asserted that "…only the weak man wishes to hurt others and see the signs of suffering." The truly powerful have no need to prove their might by hurting or oppressing others. And in regards to personal power: "Whole nations have fallen victim to criminal dictators because they could not find the inner power to act autonomously. Grown-up children never break the bonds to the parents because they could not endure the wrath of their frustrated tyranny and possessiveness." Dr. Edward Edinger

The dangerous demagoguery and callous behavior of our current White House apprentice and his administration not only undermine the entire democratic process, but these bureaucrats vitiate the trusted offices they serve. This behavior confirms a self-serving plutocracy that cares not about the people it is paid and sworn to serve. With respect to all those who condone and support this dark and dangerous behavior, I will quote a friend from another troubled country when describing the politics there: "You get the kind of leaders that you deserve." But still, avoidance and denial are powerful defenses.

Maybe one day, like so many others, the affluent and their sycophants will discover the tragedy of being outwardly successful but inwardly unsatisfied, and that those who become so obsessed with success, have already failed. These are the types of intelligent people that are just smart enough to be dangerous. The wealthy, along with their corporate media, learned long ago that the most effective way of rendering the poor and the middle class harmless is to teach them to want to imitate the rich. In the end, the downfall of so many begins with a lack of self-awareness, self-scrutiny and self-honesty.

These questionable leaders came into power by way of collective thinking -mass mentality. Their followers carry the same anger, hate and fear that lurks deep within their incorrigible leaders. And when married to a lack of independent, critical thinking it is a recipe for failure and disaster. Important research of the "primitive mind," by the anthropologist Lucien Levy Buhl suggests that this collective thinking is *unconscious mutual identification*, which is also the basis of mob mentality.

By now, the unending falsehoods and hyperbole of our leaders are well-known and well-documented. In extensive studies of history and human behavior it seems abundantly clear that our society itself is supportive of and conducive to arrogance, violence, narcissism, toxic consumerism, blind patriotism, military madness and neuroses of every kind. And those who would support the distorted mindset of conflict and chaos only serve to prove just how powerful denial and avoidance really are. Our enemies need not fear, for we appear to be destroying ourselves from within. This was also a public prediction made by former Soviet leader, Nikita Khrushchev, also not a big advocate of freedom and egalitarianism. Some people in this country have even been persuaded to surrender their rights voluntarily. Surprisingly, it was Benjamin Franklin who proclaimed that, "Those who would give up freedom for safety, deserve neither."

The tragic irony is that some of these sanctimonious souls are willing to harm or even kill someone to prove that they are right, or that they are free –having little or no concern for human life other than their own. And yet we must find a way to awaken from our apathetic slumber, rise above the madness, and try to leave the world a little better place for our children. We often speak of love and the value of freedom, but we do not seem to have a clear understanding of either concept. Shakespeare once declared that "No prisons are more confining than those we know not we are in."

Nothing has really changed in our modern era -it is **we** who must change- and yet the very source of our problems, the human psyche, is never considered on a serious level as we continue to look for the answers outside of ourselves. Especially applicable here, is Einstein's definition of insanity.

The neglect of our deeper selves begins in our family history and its consequences ripple down through the generations. When a family friend was asked to describe the current President's father, she simply stated that he was "a machine," essentially, in a divided world where there were only winners and losers and where there was little love and affection shown in the household. And when questioned about his brother's early death his dispassionate reply was that his brother was "just not a killer," a disturbing but telling response. Among his mother's laments, she was reported to have commented that she was very disappointed in her son. More often, damaged young boys become troubled old men.

"Children are so deeply involved in the psychological attitudes of their parents that it is no wonder that most of the nervous disturbances in childhood (and in adulthood) can be traced back to a disturbed psychic atmosphere in the home." -C.G. Jung (parentheses mine)

For a child, the internalized and deeply ingrained patterns of these early and vital relationships have at their core the central theme of powerlessness. The routinely experienced sense of being powerless and at the mercy of the moods and unpredictable emotions of the primary caretakers compels the child to identify with those caregivers in an effort to survive. And, aware of it or not, what child hasn't experienced a sense of having no power or say-so in some situation?

There are examples that would support the notion of the survival instinct that is carried over into adulthood, e.g. "The Stockholm Syndrome," where adult captives not only helped their captors but also joined them in their violent and dangerous behavior. A similar example can be found in the abduction of Patty Hearst and her voluntary involvement with the Symbionese Liberation Army. Followers of the Jim Jones cult in Guyana were so submissive to his power and charisma that more than 900 people committed mass suicide. Succumbing to power can have very unpleasant consequences.

These self-protective strategies are generated by the psyche, develop in the personality and are used as a method of survival by their host. Some of this behavior is simultaneously used as a way of managing the anxiety that also occurs in these situations. Underneath the most common and unconscious strategies here is the idea that people feel powerless. Then, fully conscious of it or not, they often choose to devote their lives to having power over others. Men driven to power and unable to see within are often dangerous, and yet always suspicious of danger in the outer world, and guns and bombs are the symbols of their fear.

This appears in the professional arena as well, where those obsessed with power are perceived as ambitious and industrious. In a society that admires productivity and aggression these behaviors are richly rewarded. People in our extroverted society know little of the value and importance of turning inward. They live from outside in, instead of from inside out, always anxious to find the answers, and the adversary, "out there."

In more intimate relationships the partner with this mindset operates in the realm of power, not love. The controlling psychology of the powerless person is to grab and hold as much power as possible. They manipulate their lives so as not to relive and replay the deep fears they felt as children. The great spiritual psychologist, Jung also declared that, "The greatest burden that children will ever bear, is to live the unlived life of their parents."

A reverse strategy is equally observable in the drive for power. The powerlessness felt by a child from someone who is a caretaker and a source of well-being, can teach a child to be pleasing, pacifying or overly-responsible for the well-being of others, and co-dependence is one such management strategy. (Hollis,1996)

In any case, the driven person is seldom content and never close to their own soul. The interesting thing about many of those with wealth and power is that they have everything they could ever want, everything it seems, but themselves. And wealth and power addicts cost this country far more than all the alcohol and drug abuse combined. "Where love reigns, there is no will to power; and where the will to power is paramount, love is lacking."   C.G.Jung

The Way We Are Headed

As we delve further into the text, we notice a more and more superior tone taken on by the authors, suggesting that the rise of a cognitive class in America is solely due to the rise of the superior, cognitive elite in this country. We are told that these people climb the ladder by just being more intelligent and talented than the rest of us. This we are told is the "triumph of the American ideal," and of course we have our own observations. We submit that when minorities and women are provided with the same opportunities they too can excel and contribute to society. From our psychological perch we have also seen that some of that cream that rises to the top can curdle. Being successful and intelligent does not necessarily bring happiness. Happiness is not a permanent state of mind and it is not measured by what we have, but by who we are, how we treat others and how we feel about ourselves. Happiness is transitory -it does not last- and it should not be the goal in life.

In fact, there are waiting rooms filled with those analysands who seemed to have it all, but suffered from dis-ease on different levels. It was the renowned professor, Joseph Campbell, who pointed out that there are many people who "climb the ladder" only to later realize that they propped it up against the wrong wall. As mentioned, one of the saddest observations to be made when working with people is to listen to those who are outwardly successful but inwardly dissatisfied. The affluent and the cognitive elite are no more immune from mental anguish and life's difficulties than the rest of us.

The book goes on to state that the country's abundance of wealth and success was made possible by twentieth century technology, "which expanded the need for people with high IQ by order of magnitude." If there is an "abundance of wealth," then there is a vast majority of people who've never seen it. Ranking and categorizing people in accordance to IQ has the tendency to have a divisive tone, even if this was not the authors' intent. And much like the elitism of the past, it also seems clear that technology has brought a large amount of wealth and success to only a favored few.

We also know that technology can and will be used for reasons that are not always of benefit to mankind. Even notable innovators like Bill Gates and Elon Musk have cautioned us about the use of Artificial Intelligence and the dangers that those who are enamored with technology, refuse to consider. The goliaths and primary benefactors of technology, like Amazon, Facebook and Google, are currently under scrutiny for data mining, facial recognition, cognitive engineering and the unethical misuse of our personal information. Their technological methods of behavior modification now endanger our entire future. They've recently received even more money from government, the military and big business to monitor every aspect of our lives. This perilous moment in our history was brilliantly outlined in the *Age of Surveillance Capitalism*, a masterful and incisive volume by Harvard professor emerita, Shoshana Zuboff.

More nefarious minds are now working to enrich themselves by collecting and using data in self-serving endeavors that will **not** change our lives for the better. This technological takeover has far reaching implications that will only serve the wealthy and the cognitive elite, who the Bell Curve exalts as deity. Noticing the dangerous path in the way that we are headed, one legislative investigator referred to these tech giants as "technology thugs." So, contrary to what the authors profess in their rhetoric, there never has been and never will be an equal place for all. Praising the (currently faltering) economic system that creates all this abundance the authors proudly proclaim this as "…a classic example of people free to respond to opportunity," as if everyone were actually provided with the same choices and opportunities. It was once noted that technology is the new sun -and it's blinding us. The dangers of biotechnology, genetic editing, coupled with greed and human error are ignored by the masses at their own peril.

Additional support for our position comes from other concerned and conscientious scientists. The respected and widely known theoretical physicist, Stephen Hawking asserted that the success of artificial intelligence "will mean the end of mankind" -he did not mince words. When interviewed about the issue, the Dean of Computer Science and Robotics at the Carnegie Mellon Institute, Andrew W. Moore stated that AI would "absolutely be used for evil purposes." Not only is it inevitable, but all signs indicate that those who would profit from the control of their fellow men have already arranged their Faustian bargain. Perhaps dispassionate scientists themselves have become automatons; time will tell. Still, the needed open and honest discussions about critical issues that should be ongoing are avoided by those who stand to gain the most. Hailed as the greatest scientist of our time, Albert Einstein made a definitive statement on the subject: "Spirit must overcome technology."

Capitalist societies like the U.S. operate within a framework that is based on the constant interplay between business and government, more often with a revolving door that allows top executives to gain an upper hand by experiencing the best of both worlds. They are allowed to use these back and forth experiences to give an advantage to government, and at the same time, provide superfluous profits to the avaricious world of big business. While this used to be done in a more clandestine fashion, it's now no holds barred. It doesn't take a magna cum laude from Harvard to determine that the ruling elites have no intention of creating a level playing field. They have no interest in being honest and helpful to the very ones who generate their revenue. They sacrifice their ethics and principles on the altar of commerce to the new gods of Profit and Gain. At this point, and without exaggeration, we can only wonder if freedom and democracy will even survive.

It is also beneficial to review a few more elitist strategies that create "abundant opportunities for everyone." A critical factor in considering all these issues is to scrutinize the mass media. It is no secret that the primary concerns for the corporate media are ratings and market share, with little concern for fairness and honesty. Largely culpable for the state of things today, the mass media no longer stands for the truth, but rather, it stands in the way of the truth. More often the corporate media serves as the cheerleader and the megaphone for the wealthy and their self-serving interests, many who proudly call themselves conservatives. One of our current state senators, one who actually tries to represent the people, accurately assessed that "the system is rigged." We propose that not only is the system rigged, but that it was bought and sold long ago -lock, stock and barrel. The *New Manifest Destiny* that is now being implemented is more perilous and threatening than people even care to face.

We know that the accumulation of wealth and excessive power has been the primary focus of elitists and their think tanks for quite some time now. We will not venture deeply into the financial state of the country, however, history will show that the economic stranglehold begins around 1914 with the inception of the Federal Reserve, where the chairman is installed by the President, but which is actually operated by wealthy elitists, banks, etc. Over 40% of the stock market itself is currently dominated by the top 1% of the most affluent. By 1981, approximately 1500 major companies listed by the New York Stock Exchange dominated both the American and the world economy. It appears that legitimized organizations like the World Trade Organization (W.T.O.), World Bank and the International Monetary Fund (IMF), the Council on Foreign Relations along with the

Federalist Society, have mostly operated in the shadows of power for quite some time. In 1844, the famous British statesman, Benjamin Disraeli wrote that "The world is governed by very different personages from what is imagined by those who are not behind the scenes." Covert gatherings like the Bilderberg meetings, established in 1954 are now more well-known collusions. Described as a capitalist cabal these powerful, elitist kingmakers will stop at nothing to impose their will and their avaricious agenda onto this country and across the globe.

More than just conspiracy theory, justice of the U.S. Supreme Court Felix Frankfurter (1939-1962) reiterated Disraeli's distressing statement when he said, "The real rulers in Washington are invisible, and exercise power from behind the scenes." One of the primary reasons that the general public doesn't know more about these key groups is that the propaganda machine, oiled by powerful elitists, works so well. Also blameworthy is our apathetic, distracted citizenry who are more enthralled with sports and pseudo-reality TV, than wanting to know the truth. So when the book we're reviewing begins to talk about fairness, the virtues of capitalism and an equal place for everyone, there are a few facts that its authors have overlooked.

While this is only the tip of the iceberg, it is important to point out that these plans and strategies are anything but fair and they display no interests for the plight of the common man whatsoever. It is then understandable how these particular authors would totally denounce egalitarianism, with its promise for genuine equality. It is also easy to understand how, at this particular time, Murray is attempting to revive and champion these ideas once again. The rhetoric about doing what's in America's best interest is in reality doing what's in the interest of the wealthy and the powerful, and it will inevitably return to haunt us all. The birds always come home to roost. The irony here is that it is the American people, not the perpetrators, that pay for the mass corruption and the unnecessary wars that are fought. And we pay that price in lives as well as purse.

Another successful method that ensures that the laws work in favor of corporate predators is the practice of lobbying, something most of us have heard about. The vacillating activity between politics and big business that was mentioned earlier involves those who lobby for corporations and then go on to work in government or vice versa. This is essentially the purchasing of politicians and legislators and it ensures that the best interests of capitalism and big business are served. While a few politicians in the past have attempted to thwart this practice, staunch supporters of this deceitful practice line their pockets and then allow the corporations themselves to craft the laws and the policies that allow them to continue their sordid behavior.

Insurance companies audaciously sit at the table while lawmakers make the rules to ensure that those companies get their way. Should we even wonder why our insurance rates are through the roof, or why some insurance is even mandated, or, why these companies are allowed to foist an array of unnecessary insurance policies onto an unwitting public, often refusing to honor their contractual obligations. The overreach of their excessive power is no secret. There is an enormous amount of money to be made from keeping people physically and mentally ill, and the elitists that profit from it have it down to a science.

The authors of The Bell Curve wax on about the benefits of capitalism and the opportunities available to all. They seem to have missed any research on deregulation and the extensive damage that it has continued to do to our country since the Reagan administration. As mentioned, his administration was also responsible for bending to the will of his corporate sponsors and de-institutionalizing the mental healthcare system. This was done behind the guise of allowing the mentally ill their independence. This was only a subterfuge that succeeded in helping insurance companies to save money, while creating widespread pauperism and despair.

All these ideas were key factors contributing to the economic collapse during the Bush years, and some good research might tell us just how far the poor and the middle class have really fallen. The current administration has gone to even further extremes with a policy of **total** deregulation, which now ensures the shameless and unabated pillaging and plundering. Where are the concerned and patriotic media outlets, curious researchers and the other purveyors of the truth? We contend that deregulation only serves to legitimize greed and corruption. Maybe these are the new "American ideals" that the authors spoke of so highly.

It is important to look at just a few more examples of the American ingenuity that would belie even the suggestion of a fair and level playing field. Other factors that contribute to the disparity and the growing poverty in this country, and that also require superior cognitive ability, are ideas like *regulatory arbitrage,* whereby corporations spend millions to hire teams of lawyers in order to avoid and circumvent rules and regulations. These rules were put into place to monitor and curb corporate greed and protect ordinary citizens, however laws mean nothing if they are not enforced.

And why are offshore tax havens for the wealthy well known but never challenged? No time is wasted taking away other peoples' property and assets when they don't pay their taxes. This practice alone costs our country billions of dollars in revenue each year, while the wealthy fight relentlessly to avoid helping the homeless and the needy. Billionaires now travel the country to buy off state and local politicians in order to cling to their assets. The stakes are so high that they are willing to spend millions of their own "dark money" to get their way. Leading economists have determined that, in the current political climate, the American economy may be in the throes of yet another collapse. We also know that the sitting President's past is riddled with allegations of tax fraud, cheating workers, racial discrimination, licentious acts and other illegal activity; old habits are hard to break and these are said to be our best and our brightest. If these leaders are not our best and our brightest, why aren't they?

In any direction we travel, we may all be headed for our own demise if everyone is not included in a true democratic process. If the same fairness in testing, and the same standards of measuring cognitive ability are not applied to those who are hired to make life and death decisions, then why is testing for the rest of us so important? History alone has shown us that some of the so-called geniuses in society are the very ones that have used their superior intellects for their own dark and self-serving purposes. History is replete with all the high-minded, charismatic men who have left a long string of corpses in their wake. It is also clear that the most horrific atrocities are committed by the most self-righteous.

It is only arrogance and elitist thinking that would attempt to equate intelligence to goodness and morality. Recruiting like-minded followers who also possess a spurious sense of entitlement and superiority is not so difficult when we consider the power of projections and our ignorance of the unconscious.

If social media, computers and the internet are the future then it is more important than ever to go inside and find out who we really are, so that we might learn to interact with each other in a fairer and humanistic way. We know that we spend our time and resources on what is most important to us. The great theologian, Paul Tillich suggested that faith is not so much about our conscious beliefs, as it is about where our "ultimate concerns" lie. If we lose our sensitivity, our compassion and our humanity along the way, then all the prosperity and intelligence in the world will not have mattered.

In the book, the authors have suggested that the cognitive elite have a hard time understanding what "ordinary people" think. It is interesting and a little sad that these superior beings can't just see themselves as ordinary people with higher IQ scores. It is also ironic that it is the kind of mentality in The Bell Curve that creates the separatist thinking that the authors are now alluding to. If as suggested, that the cognitive elite truly have a feeling of being isolated from the rest of society, then exactly who created those boundaries? And are those boundaries impenetrable? Cognitive elites may be a class unto themselves, however this will not save them from the same fate as the rest of us. Maybe they could expand their lexicon to include simple terms like tolerance, fairness, compassion and acceptance.

At the core of accepting people for who they are is being able to accept ourselves. Instead of teaching people to like themselves for who they are, billions are made from people who are convinced that they need to have more and be more, and not be content with who they really are. To be loved for the very ones we are is a natural need that begins in early childhood. More often, parents cannot provide us with everything we need at the different stages of our development. When these needs go unmet, it can create distrust, self-loathing and behavior that is often critical and exclusive of others. People have choices to allow others into their lives or not, to separate themselves from others or not, there is no mandate. Our choices and behavior also rely on how we choose to view things. Those who separate themselves from others and then feel alienated may be suffering from self-inflicted wounds.

On page 514 we are again bludgeoned with the notion that wealth is somehow equivalent to superior intelligence. Sometimes this might be accurate, but wealth can also be obtained by different means. If, as mentioned, the incestuous relationship between cognitive elites and the affluent has become popular, it is only in the shared interest of money and power. Capitalism has two essential components: market competition and the pursuit of profit. Max Weber once declared that the most outstanding characteristic of capitalism was production "for the pursuit of profit, and ever renewed profit." Capitalism has indoctrinated people to see the drive for profit and gain as morally acceptable, normal and socially desirable. Playing into what we know about competition and the ego, it is easy to understand how people can get caught up in their own self-serving agendas, forsaking all others. Intelligence can play a major role in accumulating money, but love and kindness require more than intelligence. As a rule, you can't teach people how to be sensitive and loving if it is not a part of their natural composition.

There is an array of intelligent people who have means and various skills, but who also display bizarre and unhealthy behavior. There are also a number of people who have inherited their fortunes, or who have not acquired wealth by their own hard work and honesty. This is less publicized due to the fact that they have the means to remain isolated and under the radar. Americans have been taught to believe that materialism is good. And the corporate media learned long ago that an effective way to manipulate people is to encourage them to covet what they can't have. The untold story is that while America's materialism and toxic consumerism are encouraged, the general population is never informed the reality that very few will live in wealth and luxury. It is then inferred that if one doesn't acquire wealth and prosperity, that this is somehow reflective of their own flaws and weaknesses, or just plain laziness.

The authors of the book "predicted" that the cognitive elite would join forces with the wealthy to control government. Not only had this already begun, but the war on poverty and the social programs that would have helped the least among us have been thwarted since day one. Author, Michael Parenti received his Ph.D. from Yale and has held guest professorships at various universities. In *Democracy for the Few (1988)*, he states clearly: "Socialization into the orthodox values of American culture is achieved not only by indoctrination but also by economic sanctions designed to punish dissent and reward political conformity." In our society we are taught to "look out for number one," and to "get ahead," at all cost. We're all taught exceptionalism, nationalism and consumerism, while the few programs that support the poor and the working class are undermined -this seems to be where we've always been headed. In this part of the book however, we also hear a bewildering concern for the underclass. These bipolar contradictions are inconsistent and misleading.

Dr. Parenti continues: "The plutocratic culture teaches us that proximity to the poor is to be shunned, while wealth is something to be pursued and admired. People who occupy privileged positions within the social hierarchy become committed to the hierarchy's preservation and hostile towards demand for greater equalization. According to one study (W. Form and J. Rytina, 1969) upper-income people were most opposed to equality of political power for all groups, while lower-

income respondents were the firmest supporters of equality."
(parentheses mine)

When we apply the concept of projection in trying to understand the meanness and hostility towards the less fortunate it is also important to remember that, while much of this behavior is conscious and intentional, the impetus for that behavior is often unconscious. When others are seen as weak or inferior it can become easy to vent our anger and frustration onto them. In the wild, the weakest of the herd is always the chosen target of predators. What often follows in the real world are actions which are not becoming that of intelligent and fair-minded people. This is the very behavior that was outlined in our description of scapegoat mentality. Other like-minded scapegoaters, often encouraged by a darker element, can then join in the fray and it isn't difficult to see how this can develop into mob mentality. This is also said to involve Bruhl's ideas of unconscious mutual identification, which is at the core of this mass mentality.

Ideas about the unconscious are generally ignored or dismissed by the scientific community. Many scientists have built their careers around ideas and theories that are considered acceptable in the scientific world and of course have their importance. We must never overlook the value of science. But the inability to shift paradigms has at times hindered our ability to move forward. A striking and familiar example is the story of Galileo Galilei, whose brilliant and well known discoveries cost him dearly. Once sponsored and supported by the Church, when his ideas conflicted with the religious beliefs of the time, he would spend the rest of his days imprisoned in his own home, even after recanting his own ideas. Misoneism was not just a problem for past civilizations.

In concluding with another callous statement made by the authors, we find it interesting when people seem be oblivious about their own actions and behavior: "Incompetent mothers are highly concentrated among the least intelligent, and their numbers are growing." So can we interpret this to mean that there is an overgrowth of less intelligent, incompetent women that should be targeted? Or maybe we could target a small portion of the billions in unpaid taxes by the wealthy, that could easily pay for the education of these women, thereby helping their children, and uplifting the entire country.

Let us hypothesize that neurotic mothers are highly concentrated among those who are considered more intelligent, or more affluent, and the number of children that have been affected by them is growing. This appears to be just as valid a theory as the above quoted statement. As indicated earlier, when parents do not deal with their own deeper issues effectively, then they inadvertently pass on their neurotic behavior to their children, and this has no socioeconomic boundaries. We are also unclear about just how these researchers have measured the incompetence of mothers, and how they successfully correlated that to their intelligence. It just seems that somewhere along the line, the authors are missing the ship that's destined to arrive, called "The Family of Man." Or perhaps, they are more captivated by the lure of the *Danse Macabre*.

The Crusade for Eugenics

"Perfection is the enemy of the good."
Voltaire

The misguided *eugenics* campaign of the twenties was predicated on the notion that the best features of human beings should be dictated by elites and those of superior intelligence, much akin to the thinking in the text we're reviewing. These ideas were promoted and popularized, and eugenic sterilization spread to 21 states in the U.S.

Pioneers of American Eugenics begin in the hallowed halls of some of our most cherished academic institutions, like Stanford University in Palo Alto. It was there where the infamous William Shockley, obsessed with ideas about IQ and race his entire life, was said to have devoted himself and his office at Stanford to the full time pursuit of white supremacy. This bloated Stanford cabal, joined to the military industrial complex at the hip, created an achievement society, where human capital became Palo Alto's main product.

With the help of powerful and like-minded people, like Herbert Hoover and others, Stanford's highly organized and systematized success factory is involved in everything from agriculture, railroads and finance, to some of our highest political offices. And to this day, Palo Alto's elitists in the Silicon Valley continue to receive exorbitant amounts of taxpayer dollars in government contracts to continue their nefarious projects, shredding the social safety net, while making themselves obscenely wealthy. Facilitating the way for predatory capitalism and world domination, these intellectual superiors have proven that intellect and education are not in the least conducive to goodness, kindness and humanitarianism.

Even Harvard University once taught eugenics classes, often based on faith and the distortions of religion. And while the idea that science can engineer better human beings is attractive to some, others aver that it is more of a scientific arrogance that seeks perfection and segregation. On a cursory level, it appears to be the need for dominance and control over others -power. On a deeper level it is also known as projection. And what is this projection essentially about? It has been likened to playing God, or identifying with a deity. And it is also part of the ego inflation to which we continually refer. The original state of affairs is in experiencing one's self as the center of the universe, and this can persist far past childhood.

A stark example of eugenic fanaticism leads us to a 1924 U.S. Supreme Court landmark decision and Buck vs. Bell, the case of Carrie Buck. Ms. Buck became the young victim of bad science and questionable cognitive testing. She was determined to be feeble-minded following the testing that determined that she suffered from low cognitive ability, and she was consequently ordered to be sterilized. The final decision to have this young woman sterilized was favored by lower court judges who determined that the practice of allowing morons to breed could no longer be tolerated. Considered brilliant and forthright, even Supreme Court Justice Oliver Wendell Holmes voted to have this poor and powerless citizen sterilized, for the betterment of American society of course.

At this point it would be important for us all to speculate by what god-like authority any individual -albeit well educated and cognitively superior- is allowed to make such vital decisions over the lives of others. It has also become clear that the social engineers that were labeling people as socially inadequate were targeting the poor, the socially disfavored and those with unacceptable disabilities. Proponents of the eugenics craze were later forced to admit their "science" was tragically flawed, and yet they continued with their obsessions in order to dominate and control their powerless and disenfranchised fellow citizens.

This dangerous ideology was not only pushed onto the poor and the voiceless, and it should awaken our conscience and give us all something to think about. When wedded with the drive for power and control, this kind of distorted thinking could potentially find anyone in its cross-hairs. To wit, the case of Ann C. Hewitt, an affluent white woman who by all standards was an otherwise healthy and well-kept woman. At the time (1936), Ann stood to inherit a substantial sum from her father's estate. The will and testimony in this matter had only one proviso: if his daughter Ann had no children at the time of the estate's disbursements, then Ann would lose her inheritance by default. His millions would then be bequeathed to her ambitious mother. Soon thereafter, her mother had her own daughter embroiled in a lengthy court battle, alleging that Ann was feeble-minded and mentally defective. In court, Miss Hewitt accused her mother of duping her into a sterilization procedure without her consent.

Part of mentioning these cases is of course to point to a more modern text that appears to have a similar ideology throughout its content. Also involved are our genuine concerns about the power that is invested in the state, that happens to consist of decision-makers who are subject to the same human weaknesses, flaws and bias as the rest of us. The consideration about sterilization in the Hewitt case could easily be seen as having the underlying motive of monetary gain. We seem to allow a great deal of authority to those who may not always have our best interest in mind. It is advisable that people know themselves, become more conscious, and understand that there are those who would gladly take our power and our choices from us, should we let them. And their theft is not always accomplished by sheer force.

Eugenic evangelists like Harry Laughlin made it his goal in life to make eugenic sterilization a household slogan. Later on, abandoned by a majority of the scientific community, his obsessive determination never wavered. The effects of his self-serving agenda, along with other distorted thinkers like Madison Grant, would spill over and inspire the likes of Adolph Hitler. Hitler would go on to enact sterilization laws in Nazi Germany modeled on the original ideas of Laughlin and Grant in the United States. Like-minded Americans proudly displayed signs and banners denouncing those who were unfortunate enough not to pass the tests that announced their human limitations. Just one glaring example of this dark thinking was a banner that simply read: "We pay the cost for the feeble-minded."

Much like modern day scientists and researchers who relentlessly strive for the unreachable promise of human perfection, these cognitively superior beings found only failure. And as mentioned earlier, some of the most sanctimonious and well-intentioned figures in history have orchestrated some of the most destructive and inhumane events on the planet. More often, attempts at non-existent perfection and the betterment of the human race have only resulted in places like Dachau and Buchenwald. In another part of their discourse, authors of the text we're observing quoted the British statesman, Edmund Burke. At this point we would like to add our own Burke quote to the mix, when he said, "All that is necessary for evil to triumph is for good men to do nothing."

Maybe now we can begin to see that the idea that women who are considered less intelligent and inferior, is closely associated to the idea that immigrants and people of color are of the same ilk. Not surprisingly, this type of thinking is more often held by the affluent and the privileged who may sincerely -albeit erroneously- believe that they are the superior beings that should rule the world, a perfect example of ego inflation. When we consider that often, at the base of this ideology is fear, anger, insecurity and self-centeredness then we might better understand that the only approach to any solutions at our betterment lie in the human psyche. Outer solutions to inner problems have been proven to be limited and relatively ineffective.

In keeping with their line of thinking, the authors then openly suggest that our government should give no helping hand to single mothers who struggle to survive. All the while we still hear no mention of corporate bailouts and exorbitant tax breaks for the wealthy. "By the people and for the people" has quickly become "by the corporations and for the wealthy." With over half of hard-working taxpayer dollars being spent on an imperialistic agenda, the truth is that the superfluous military budget greatly contributes to draining us dry. Dr. King referred to these self-destructive martial practices as "the madness of militarism." We would welcome the research that accurately reflects the amount of money spent on corporate welfare and the military, versus the money spent on social welfare programs and help for the truly needy.

At the same time and as mentioned earlier, we are aware of the fact that it is generally the instinct of mothers to nurture and protect their offspring. This is not based on IQ levels or socioeconomic status, although the privileged irrefutably have an advantage when it comes to the nurturing part. To vilify and condemn unwed mothers for their IQ scores and then sentence them to a life of poverty and deprivation is to avoid facts and deny reality. It supports the arguments for a better understanding of scapegoating and misogyny, while exposing those who have lost their compassion and their humanity.

Furthermore, if we are truly concerned about where we are headed, then it is impossible to see other human beings as expendable and a "future drag" on our economy. All this dehumanizing double-speak has nothing to do with a true concern for America's best interest. We are all Americans, and as such, we are all connected and deserving of each other's help. And if one person fails, then I too have failed.

Addressing some of the unfulfilled predictions on page 523, we do see children being torn from the arms of their parents, but it appears like our elected leaders support this despicable practice and do nothing to rectify the situation. Perhaps the lives of migrant children are of less value than other more favorable children. As we know, the child refugees that are currently entering this country are being criminalized, separated from their parents and thrown into prison camps. Now accommodating thousands of refugee children, our leaders in all their wisdom, have seen fit to psychologically damage children rather than help them. This fiasco is done behind the pretext of safety and security, while the American conscience lies dormant. We've already learned that most of these refugees seeking legal asylum are fleeing from violence, starvation and oppression, apparently seeing imprisonment and mistreatment as their better option.

A prediction by the authors that "the homeless will vanish" has not materialized either, and homelessness increases with little or no concern displayed by our leaders. But then, when researchers and elites portray these people as a useless drag on our society, as well as undeserving of our help, how does this contradictory statement even become possible? We've already talked about those who are caught in poverty's despair, and how they are merely victims of the heartless system that created them, forever the scapegoats of a lost and empty society.

On page 524, author predictions of increasingly strict policing tactics have excelled beyond the authors' wildest dreams. The authoritarian *police state* is now in full swing with racial profiling and with minorities, who are mostly black, being executed by the the very authorities that are paid to serve and protect them. The cries for justice and equality fall on deaf ears. And again, more draconian measures of punishment against the oppressed have been proven to be ineffective, consequently exposing our citizens to more and more crime and violence. These failing strategies are encouraged by the corporate media and by those who support an outdated, punitive mindset. One can only conclude that at some time in their lives, some of the people with this thinking faced harsh discipline themselves. Meanwhile, the vital contributing factors of poverty and inequality are being ignored and avoided by those who were hired to fix the problems. However, their prisons for profit are thriving. It was once noted that justice without mercy is only tyranny.

The self-fulfilling prophecies made some twenty-five years ago like "stop and frisk," intrusive surveillance, electronic ankle bracelets and other tactics were in large part due to the ideology that is supportive of a fearful, oppressive, authoritarian state. Obviously, where we are headed is precisely where the authors wanted us to go. Admit it or not, we are now witnessing the end of independence, privacy, our civil liberties, the end of our democracy, and the rapid decline of a once great nation.

And alas, the authors of The Bell Curve are correct in saying that the so-called underclass has grown, but incorrect in defining the underclass as the cognitive elite. It seems deceitful to frame the callous engineers of our current crisis as an underclass. Any serious or careful analysis of the current crisis America now faces would support the idea that this was intended and well planned by those who consider themselves to be intellectually superior. Believing that they are right, just and deserving, they invite us to join them on their moribund march to nowhere. Some psychologists have suggested that we are masters of self-delusion.

A Place for Everyone

Struck by the title of this final chapter, we could only wonder if its co-author had noticed that what it infers is so inconsistent with the rest of the book. It seems difficult **not** to be credulous about the content and purpose of the ideas that Murray and his supporters continuously attempt to reinforce.

We also know that the ideas of democracy that were derived from our cultural ancestors have been distorted and misused far beyond their original designs. As time changes things, so must our notions of what has existed in the past, however some things might still be worth holding on to. It was Heraclitus who proclaimed that the only thing of permanence was change. The initial ideas of some of these great thinkers originated some twenty-five hundred years ago, and yet our human flaws and weaknesses remain unchanged. For example, arrogance and greed (i.e. hubris and concupiscence) were transgressions that were also denounced and punished by Olympian law. In American culture they have become acceptable and even commonplace.

Moreover, we do not live in Greece, Rome or the Asian subcontinent, places that thrived centuries ago. And while we should maintain some degree of respect and admiration for all cultures, Athenian democracy itself was rife with tyranny, slavery, violence and oppression. This was said to have facilitated the rise of the aristocracy, who were said to have oppressed country farmers as well as urban artisans. In fact, according to historians, it was the economic prosperity of Athens married to an imperialistic agenda, which caused the increasing friction with Sparta. This eventually led to the Peloponnesian War in which Athens was soundly defeated. So it seems clear that the lust for wealth and power has been instrumental in the downfall of some of the richest and most powerful civilizations in the world.

And maybe it's true that we've not been perceptive enough to have learned from history. Taught less and less in our schools, lessons in history, the arts and culture have been replaced with courses in marketing, finance and business. John F. Kennedy once remarked that "A country with no past is a country with no future." The irony is palpable. In order to know where we're going, it is vitally important to know where we've been.

It is also important to note that the highly intellectual class in Greece became quite concerned with the defense of the plutocracy of their day, namely the class of corporate lawyers. So while wealthy leaders were ostensibly upholding the laws and justice, and were purportedly pious and moral, they appear to have been subverting ancient beliefs. It is believed that in all likelihood, they were actually attempting to destroy the democracy of their day. The parallels here are remarkable and hopefully more than obvious. But then, I'm sure there's a game, or a game-show, on somewhere.

There is some basis in fact for the authors' statement that not all men are created equal, however it appears that it is the value that **we** attach to people and their differences that affects how we see others, and it is more of a choice. Maybe what the founding fathers of this great nation saw in their proposals of defacto egalitarianism, was the fact that we are all beings of the same species -we're all human. As mentioned earlier in our text, DNA evidence proves that we are far more alike than we are different and yet elitist thinkers and leaders have always found a way to use our differences and our emotions to capitalize on those differences as a means of accessing and maintaining power. Along with violence and mendacity, these are the trademarks of fascism.

If we choose to focus on our differences, then this of course will contaminate our attitudes and our views of anyone else who is different. It is also ludicrous to allow someone else to define our reality. At a time when shameless mendacity and dangerous demagoguery rule our politics, it seems even more important to see past our differences and work toward the common good. It is more beneficial to those who perpetuate conflict and inequality to maintain fear and divisiveness. These strategies are how fortunes are made and empires are built. If we can't unite and work together, then divided, we will surely fall.

Selective quotes from philosophers like Thomas Hobbes on page 529 are also interesting to talk about. Hobbes' basic argument was that the only way to secure a civil society is through the complete (and universal) submission to the absolute authority of a sovereign. The selection of this particular philosopher says a lot about who we choose to believe. This hearkens back to an earlier discussion about individuals who choose their beliefs based on their own character and their own frame of reference. On the one hand, while denying free will, Hobbes was unlike other defenders of despotic government in that he held that all men were "naturally equal." In his absolutist philosophy there were only two choices for human society: anarchy or monarchy (his preference, the latter).

This either/or mentality typifies the psychic split that we propose exists, not only in leaders, but in most people we know and in every walk of life. Extreme "all or nothing" thinking facilitates perpetual war and conflict in the outer world, while it is the unending battle in the inner world that is never addressed, or even acknowledged. In the East, a different philosophy is taught. While we greatly respect Eastern philosophies and practices, we would also caution that it is difficult to heal a Western wound with an Eastern remedy. A key thing to point out about the differences is that Western perception is rooted in the duality (twoness) of life, while in the East is the insight that transcends duality. So the Westerner has an opposing view of things like good and evil, which creates an entirely different way of living. The occidental societies were steeped in traditions and beliefs that differ greatly from our Eastern brothers and sisters. Nevertheless, it is always wise to be eclectic in these matters, as we believe that everyone has something to bring to the table, and we can all learn from each other.

In the East it is believed that good and evil exist, however it is unnecessary to hold one position over the other. The belief is that it is more prudent to travel the middle road. This middle path between fear and desire is referred to as the Tao. Western thinking makes it much more difficult to find a place that is in-between, essentially perpetuating the struggle between good and evil. The constant movement between two extremes is essentially the sway between opposites that turns up in the stories and mythology of many different cultures. In politics, it involves moving too far left or too far right and this is considered as an unhealthy balance. It is reflected in the sometimes unfair and even mean-spirited policies that we see being proposed and enacted everywhere, but it's all seen as being outside ourselves.

If we heed the messages of wisdom in dreams and ancient myth, they can teach us how to live our lives in ways that logic and reason have not been able to convey. It is said that the intellectual life engages the mind, and the symbolic life engages the soul. We also believe that it may be time for the marriage of Western pragmatism and Eastern philosophy.

At this time, it would be helpful to return to a psychological approach to explain why we believe that these psychological elements are just as important to understand as our cognitive ability. We believe that a basic understanding of *the opposites* can lead to a better understanding of ourselves. We also suggest that we are creatures of the opposites and that thinking alone is not enough to reach the deeper balance that so many seem to be yearning for. We believe that it is in holding to the tension of the opposites that we are allowed a chance at healing and repose. Trying to avoid our own dismal states becomes a form of suffering itself, because we frantically seek to be happy and carefree, while never really being at home with ourselves.

We know that even when something good enters our lives it can become one-sided in our continuous desire to maintain that good feeling, and in times of joy we have the tendency to ignore or avoid any opposing state. Since no one can be happy all the time, then something more dark and negative can sneak in. "What goes up must come down." What is one of the most difficult things to learn is that when we hold on to the darkness, instead of running away, we are presented with an opportunity at real transformation. So powerful are the forces of the psyche when entering those depths that a weak or fragile ego should proceed with caution. When we find ourselves in these dark places, intellectualizing can prove to be useless. What no one in a hedonistic society wants to hear is that it is precisely through suffering that we find out who we really are. Swiss analyst, Marie Louise von Franz has stated clearly that it is **only** through suffering that we find ourselves -there is no way around it. If this were a simple and easy process, then as trendiness goes, everyone would want to do it.

When we take a careful look around we can see the opposites everywhere. In an earlier segment we briefly discussed a concept posed by the Danish Nobel laureate, Neils Bohr and his *Theory of Complimentarity*, which essentially proposes that opposite elements complement each other. Ideas of *antinomy* have always been met with bewilderment, although the admixture of the masculine and the feminine is seen as far back as the Greeks in hermaphroditic symbolism, as well as in alchemical images. This is all neatly dismissed as pseudoscience, and a valuable symbolic understanding is lost.

What would darkness be without the light; hot without cold; up without down? What would the sun be without the moon, and the masculine without the feminine? What kind of meaning would they even hold? These are just a few of the pairs of opposites to be considered. Examples of the opposites abound and in a more lyrical comparison it has been said that, "God is a sea of grace **and** a lake of fire."

In Analytical psychology, the concept of a deity and spirituality are not forsaken because of scientific knowledge. Gods are a reality in the hearts and minds of most cultures the world over, and as the adept psychiatrist Jung carefully pointed out, it is just as foolish to try to prove that there is a god, as it is to try to prove that there isn't one.

The ineffable mystery is just that, a great mystery, and no amount of science or statistics can unravel the mystery or fully explain it. The conjoining of a scientific approach with a more spiritual approach to life is neither new nor far-fetched, and at one point the church itself strongly supported scientific endeavors.

In both life and analysis, it is the ongoing interplay of opposites that often creates the dynamic tug of war that we experience more often than we'd like. That push and pull that we experience internally can carry a great deal of energy, which can often lead to outer conflict, both at home and abroad. We confidently assert that the nucleus of that conflict lies within, and this becomes more evident as we take our inner world more seriously. As the old comic strip character Pogo once observed, "We have seen the enemy, and they is us."

In an absolutist, one-sided mindset, we see the conflict manifested as war and fighting. It has been said that war is the failure of human beings to truly be human, and we continue to assert that the real battle is going on inside us. It is a one-sided stance that can quickly turn into its opposite, as observed in clinical settings and in the outer world. This is said to first occur in the psyche as described earlier. So powerful are these inner images that they can lead to behavior and actions that are damaging and sometimes devastating to others and to ourselves. So if we truly seek a place for everyone, it is our contention that the unity begins within each of us.

Returning to Analytical Psychology, we read an extraordinary statement written some sixty years ago that still resonates today:

"Today humanity, as never before, is split into two irreconcilable halves. The psychological rule says that when an inner situation is not made conscious, it happens outside as fate. That is to say, when the individual remains undivided and does not become conscious of his inner contradictions, the world must perforce act out the conflict and be torn into opposite halves."

C.G. Jung, 1959

Before returning to the text we digress, and interject with other ideas that we believe are relevant and that also provide us with a psychological window by which to capture a different view. We see the need to emphasize the value and importance of things like mythology and how it relates to our lives. It teaches us how to live within, and how to live in the outer world. History has shown us that all civilizations begin with a narrative, a story. At the time of his death, Joseph Campbell was considered one of the world's foremost authorities on mythology. He taught that myths have built civilizations, informed religions and guided people in how to live their lives. One of the important things to bear in mind is that myth is about the transformation of consciousness, something that science eschews. Campbell also taught that myth opens us up to a dimension of mystery that underlies all forms. Without this we are more aligned with a materialistic and programmatic life and tend to live for things outside ourselves. We are of the opinion that this greatly contributes to the emptiness, fear and dispassion that we see everywhere, in spite of all our intelligence.

We use the writers of the text we are reviewing as an example of those who are living in terms of a system. A person then essentially becomes an agent of the state. When this happens then people identify with a role and are not developing their humanity. This is in part what we encounter when dealing with a stoic, rigid mindset. Campbell likened the state itself to a machine. He noted that when man took up a stick or a stone that this was the beginnings of a machine; taking outer nature to use for our service. He then asked the incisive question: Will the machine serve man, or will the machine crush man? (*The Power of Myth*, 1991)

A sway to the opposites was referred to as the *enantiodromia* by the Greeks, and it often appears in their mythology, which attempted to guide them on their inner journey. The Greeks are our cultural ancestors and theirs was the first civilization to express ideas and articulate specific images that are central to the human psyche. They were the first to step out of the primordial abyss that they named *Chaos (khaos)*, which now plays an important role in modern science as well. When we talk about *cosmos (kosmos)*, then we are speaking of *order* and the world defined as an orderly, harmonious whole. Back in the third or fourth century B.C., Euhemerus began the suspicion of mythology when he posited that myths were all tales derived from historical events. This was the beginning of the idea that myths were merely fictional stories, and the great loss of their deeper psycho-logical meaning carried on into the modern era.

The great danger of modern thinking is that Greek philosophy is seen as only abstract stories from the past, more-or-less lifeless structures. And although there are various ideas about mythology, suffice it to say that when seen psychologically, the powerful images found in myths and dreams have the ability to take us beyond the limitations of our conscious understanding.

A group of young children was once questioned about what they believed myths were. With answers ranging from stories that were untrue, to just our imagination, a young boy stood up and stated that myths were stories that were not true on the outside, but true on the inside. Myth and lore can act as guideposts for our path in life, and if understood symbolically, they carry the possibility for gifting our lives with meaning and bringing us into harmony.

As their references to the founding fathers continue, the authors seem to be choosing sources that are in support of inequality -an unequal "place for everyone." On page 528 the authors of The Bell Curve have suggested that their readers think of equality as an ideal. By definition an ideal is something that is regarded as a standard or measure of perfection or excellence, even absolute perfection. Throughout the text this is hinted as an acceptable American value, at least to those like-minded thinkers. And while it may be desirable to do our best, striving for an elusive state of perfection can quickly lead to frustration and disappointment. Plato himself once exclaimed that perfection was best left for the gods.

When attempts are made to apply the standards of perfection to any individual, we can rest assured that that individual will always come up short. Even the ancients understood that perfection is an illusion and happiness is ephemeral.

The dictionary defines equality as: "The state or instance of being equal; especially the state of enjoying equal rights, as political, economic and social." To frame equality as some lofty ideal allows us to use perfection as a tool of measurement. Not only is this a high bar to set, but at the same time, it ignores our similarities and our commonality as human beings. It also conveniently overlooks the fact that we are all imperfect. As an old comedy sketch once amusingly pointed out, "I think we're all Bozos on this bus." We are all flawed, and in the world of counseling it is believed that a majority of us are the *walking wounded*.

We also know that when people aren't aware that they operate from a place inside, then their own feelings of fear and insecurity can easily cause them to project their darkness onto innocent parties. This behavior is found at work, in school, at home and even in church where others end up taking the brunt of our unconscious darkness.

Even with the best education money can buy and all the intellectualizing that we can do, we can run, but we can **never** hide from ourselves.

It is here that we share some wisdom from the ancient Gnostic gospels. Discovered in 1945 in upper Egypt, the Nag Hammadi texts are believed to be the hidden sayings of Jesus. From the Gospel of Thomas, we read the following most profound statement: "If you bring forth what is within you, what you bring forth will save you. If you do not bring forth what is within you, what you do not bring forth will destroy you."

Moreover, the ethical teachings of Christianity and the Christ have always presented a problem to their followers. If we accept the above premise regarding illusory perfection, then those good people who strive for total perfection will eventually find themselves in a moral quandary consisting of their own ethical standards conflicting with reality, an experience that is far from perfect. A simple example might elucidate: Jesus was a man of love and peace who denounced killing no matter the reason. This is even a basic tenet of Mosaic law, "Thou shalt not kill." And yet mothers and fathers and those professed believers of the word, are now presented with the choice of whether or not to put their sons in harm's way during a time of war. We might reason that this decision will be based on their love of country versus their love of faith. Or, couched in another way, does the love of their children override their sense of patriotism? This appears to be a very personal choice.

Some mothers seem ever so willing to sacrifice their children to a war that may not actually be fought for the reasons given by their leaders and the media. Our purpose here is to demonstrate that these major decisions involving human life are not based solely on intelligence and cognitive ability. We know that for some, the reasons we go to war are important, but they may not be clear at the time. And later, we sometimes learn that the reasons provided to us at first aren't always valid and forthright. So it seems that these vital decisions are made with something more than intelligence and idealism.

The inner conflict that arises in these various situations is seldom seen as a dynamic struggle of the opposites within, but it is often described as a feeling of being "torn apart," "divided" or being "ripped in two." Here especially, the choices and decisions that we make are better served by knowing ourselves on a deeper level. The balance or imbalance we may experience is usually reflected in the outer world. Inasmuch as it is possible, the wisdom here is to bridge the gap and reconcile our inner differences. We do know that when these inner images and their messages are ignored, then the gap only widens and we may create a more harmful situation. The answers lie within is not just a trite cliché and this is where the intellect is there to help us. It has been our conviction all along that it is only a balance of conscious and unconscious elements that can give us a chance at inner peace and outer harmony. And this involves both thinking and feeling.

Even in jury trials, after the physical evidence and witness testimony are presented, the jury convenes to make their final decision. Often times, particularly in controversial cases or close calls, it is striking to discover that the jury will more often make the final decision of guilt or innocence based -not solely on their intellect- but on their emotions. This is well known to seasoned attorneys and is demonstrated in the persuasive power of their closing arguments. In conjunction with our earlier discussion, we propose that the feeling function is just as important as the function of thinking. Thinking informs us about what the thing is and feelings appear to provide us with a value judgment about that thing, which is more often rendered from a deeper place.

Moving on in the text, we find references to the great philosopher John Locke. Again we are reminded that these ideas are more often seen through our own subjective lens. The value of philosophy is not that it provides us with all the answers, but that it helps us to formulate and to ask the right questions. John Locke's philosophy, as it appears in *The Essay,* has certain merits and other demerits. Both of these qualities were said to have been useful, however the demerits were such "only from a theoretical standpoint." Locke was said to have always been sensible and "always willing to sacrifice logic rather than become paradoxical." Some of the so-called strange consequences of his general principles he refrained from addressing, thereby making him irritating to some logicians and proof of his sound judgment to more pragmatic observers. (Bertrand Russell, 1945)

In fact, many of the ideas and theories acquired from the philosophers of yore have proven useful, while others have become philosophically outdated. Choosing what fits for us is more often about personal preference, and it is possible for our values and beliefs to change. As Heraclitus also noticed, while sitting by the banks of a flowing river, "Everything is in flux."

Here we insert the idea that paradox is helpful to our position about the opposites even though in its ambivalence it may seem frightening to those who want concrete, unequivocal answers. We suggest that it was not only Locke that was resistive to this way of thinking. Paradox itself is the condition where things oppose each other; where we are given a unique opportunity to entertain two contradictory ideas, and give them both equal attention and value. Also related to our ideas is the unorthodox proposition that it is the balance of opposite forces that carries the potential to make us whole, and it is certainly applicable to our discussion. We contend that without being able to make this paradigm shift most people will spend their energy, and much of their lives, supporting the warfare within. But while a large amount of energy is wasted by people opposing their own situations, transferring our energy from opposition to paradox is a huge leap in our modern way of thinking.

In closing this section, the use of philosophers and statesmen in an effort to support questionable and longstanding American ideals does not seem to align itself with the notion of "an equal place for everyone." The virtuous qualities of past thinkers are implicit and the contributions they made are impressive even today. However, we are defined more by our actions than we are by our words. The first obvious thing we notice is the fact that much of this early prosperity was built on the backs of slaves and other minorities, with little if any concern shown for their humanity. While some of these statesman displayed fine qualities and a genuine concern for the ideals of freedom and equality, their interests in wealth and commerce sometimes superseded their lofty ideals and the documents they crafted.

Having helped to frame the Constitution, James Madison also expressed his grave concerns about factionalism and polarization bringing down the Republic. In modern times, this bears a striking resemblance to our current situation where conflict and divisiveness continue to prevent unison both in the political world and in the public sphere. Madison's earlier remarks about government protecting the interests of the wealthy, reflected the thinking of his colleagues and set the tone for the unmovable sentiment that still echoes throughout the hallowed halls of Congress. And like many to come, his presidency would be marred by yet another war (War of 1812).

The authors then refer to Thomas Jefferson and much has been much written about our esteemed third president. Of course, along with his most notable accomplishments, were the drafting of the Declaration of Independence, the Louisiana Purchase and the Tripolitan War (1801-1805). However, even with his intelligence and high-minded virtue he harbored some significant human flaws. Seemingly one of the original egalitarians, it is well known that he was also a proponent of slave labor which was essentially how many affluent estates were allowed to thrive and flourish. It is also known that while proclaiming that slavery corrupted both slave and master, Jefferson sired several children by his personal slave, Sally Hemings. While keepers of the flag have tried to dispute these claims, both DNA and historical evidence have since confirmed their authenticity.

The resolve of those who cling to nostalgia and an unsavory past have them continuing to refute even science and history, although the former has its limits and the latter is usually written by the winners. The new recorders of events have only become more sophisticated, with their use of sensationalizing, selective focus and the omission of facts. The disseminating of information and misinformation is now in the hands of internet entrepreneurs and social media giants who gather and misuse our information to misguide us towards a place that the founding fathers never dreamed of. So jeopardized is our future, and so confused and misled are we, that we turn to the "ten thousand things" for constant distractions.

In some recent polls most Americans professed the belief in a deity, although this is not evidenced by the loving of their enemies, or even by the loving of their neighbors. There are many decent and caring people of faith, and despicable behavior can be seen on all sides. However, there are some believers in a faith built on love and charity that would have more success at proselytizing if they acted more Christ-like and looked more redeemed. Some on-line commentary even indicates that some people believe that God meant for them to be wealthy. This is where using selective hermeneutics to rationalize one's materialism makes avarice possible. Perhaps they overlooked the passage: "You cannot be the slave of both God and money (Luke 16:13)." Selecting biblical passages to serve one's own needs and wants is not a new practice and it is even seen by some as acceptable. Even going back to the 16th century, the insightful Shakespeare proclaimed, "The devil can cite scripture to his own purpose."

Still driving hard to the net of inequality, authors of the Bell Curve appear to be strongly discouraging readers away from a more equal society and towards what could only be considered as a separatist, authoritarian world where we are judged and treated by our IQ scores, socioeconomic status and skin color. And yet the surviving author seems bewildered by the firestorm and controversy that his ideas created. On page 532 we read: "To reduce inequality of condition, the state must impose greater and greater uniformity." It seems like it is the inequality itself that is the condition that must be reduced, and it must be changed in a meaningful way. This does not occur by forcing everyone to be like everyone else. Harmony is never reached when everyone sings on the same note.

With this type of thinking, it is not surprising some twenty-five years later to hear leaders that still support American exceptionalism and white nationalism. The basic tenets of Nazism were nationalism, militarism and totalitarianism. Those who share in this way of thinking are in the company of other fascist leaders like Benito Mussolini, who was executed by partisans in Italy. This pathology then spilled over into another country to infect the despot in Germany who ended up taking his own life. The pandemic then spread and contributed to the nationalist leadership of the dictator, Francisco Franco in Spain. We know that this dangerous disease is currently being revived in Europe, and its dark ideology is now infecting our own country. Is what we are seeing a sway to the opposites, and are we becoming what we've hated?

Using language like "the perversions of egalitarianism," and "the defects in egalitarianism" expose an express desire to denounce the political, economic and social freedom and equality that **is** egalitarianism. We believe that these should be well thought out personal choices. Wasn't the American Revolution fought in an effort to gain freedom and independence from our motherland? The basic core of fascism, which Americans have denounced and even fought against, would deny the freedom and equality that we all claim to cherish. At the core of fascism is a self-inflating ideology that leads to the establishment of a particular authoritarian political system. Perhaps the basic question here is: Do people prefer freedom and independence, or, do they prefer autocratic leadership? And moreover, shouldn't the final choice be left to *we the people*, rather than to corporations, elitists, and politicians, who have their own self-serving agendas? It seems to us that it's a simple choice, and maybe it's time for all of us to make a stand. Our politicians are elected to protect and serve the rights and freedom of people, not to thwart and oppress them.

Unpacking all of the misleading and deleterious comments in The Bell Curve can be challenging. Some of their so-called predictions were actually recommendations that had already been taken up by their conservative supporters and the elected officials who they favored. Strict policing methods, assignment of the poor to chosen areas, social control and the "custodial state" all clearly indicated where these authors were really headed. The latter technique is made remarkably clear in a statement made in the last chapter: "...by *custodial state*, we have in mind a high tech and more lavish version of the Indian reservation for some substantial minority of the nation's population, while the rest of America tries to go about its business." A lavish Indian reservation is a contradiction in terms, and sounds more like a concentration camp with perks. Real American natives were relegated to abject poverty. This is a telling statement that shines a light on the "place for everyone" else that the authors obviously yearn for. By this time, the apathy and animosity towards those seen as expendable should come as no surprise. This cold and calculated remark leaves no doubt about the authors' intentions.

We do agree however with the authors' notion that callous people should be allowed to speak openly about their prejudice and animosity, with no political correctness -then at least kind and caring people would know who to avoid. Allowing hate speech is a part of the new American politics and, "the freedom to act" that's spoken of in the book, is more like the freedom to act out.

On page 534 the authors now say that they are "enthusiastic about diversity," while not actually being big fans of equality under the laws themselves. What comes to mind here is that if some Americans could be trusted to be fair and kind, then there would be no need for laws that ban discrimination and hate crimes. Further on, we're told that "... it used to be easier for people who are low in ability to find a valued place than it is now," suggesting that there were better times for people who were not so smart. We wonder precisely how the authors' writing created "a valued place" for the less fortunate then or now.

It is easy to see that technology and machines are displacing workers in America. If there were real concerns for workers, those who control the power and the resources would see the value in supporting widespread education that would end up benefiting workers, businesses and the country as well. And if there was a genuine concern for our culture, then a well-rounded education would replace the modern training mills that are narrowly focused and keep their customers in debt. So while wages, benefits and workers' rights are are decreasing, so then is the American way of life and economic opportunity. This would, by extension, also mean an even more dismal prognosis for those with lower cognitive ability.

The next show of concern for our country is found in the statement that "something vital and important has drained out of American communities." It has been observed that trust, cohesiveness and tolerance are seen less and less in our communities. Many now believe that much of the fear and divisiveness we are now witnessing is actually being instilled with malevolent intentions. It is also important to note that when the authors talk about the "stuff of life that is being stripped away from our neighborhoods," it is fair treatment and programs that help to lift people up and give them a shred of dignity that **are** "the stuff."

Camouflaged in double-speak, the next blatant statements are also an indication of the direction desired by our authors. "Government policy can do much to foster the vitality of neighborhoods by trying to do less for them." An interesting pseudo-solution is presented in directing government policy to help our weakest citizens by doing less for them. We must also question precisely which neighborhoods are being left out in the cold with even less. The politicians that we hire are given the power to create policies that are in best interest of all the people, and not just those that help big business and the affluent. The laissez-faire policy decisions, which began with conservative politics decades ago have resulted in a lowered standard of living for many people, as well as an increase in the political corruption and malfeasance that we see today. It is well known by now that poverty and deprivation facilitate an increase in crime, violence, addictions and depression. It is the job of government to govern -fairly. Benign neglect and apathy are the choices of those who gain more by helping less.

In *Simplifying the Rules* (p. 541) the double-talk is even more apparent, when we're told that the U.S. is guided "by rules that are congenial to people with high IQ's and that make life more difficult for everyone else." Throughout their text we've been bombarded with the idea that it is only the highly intelligent that are deserving and prudent. If this is true, then those more intelligent people are the very ones who could change the rules and make life easier for everyone else, not harder.

It's easy to see from this statement that smarter people actually do make life harder for others, and there is plenty of evidence to suggest that they have no problem about becoming more prosperous while their lessers struggle. Deny it all they like, the cognitive elite benefit by making rules that are often one-sided and unfair; it is part of their historical legacy.

Deregulation for instance is the elimination of laws and rules that would protect the average American from corporate corruption and exploitation. This political ruse only serves corporations and the wealthy. While ostensibly a tool to free up markets, create jobs and improve peoples' lives, it's consequences have been devastating to a work force that has only seen less gainful employment with less worker's rights and benefits, and again, a lowered standard of living. Fudging the numbers of the employed to include temporary and part-time work, and ignoring jobs that don't pay a living wage, makes the statistics look good for political highwaymen. Subsequent to all of the above, the boasting and hyperbole of politicians and media about the current economic boom only supports our position; bottom line is that the so-called "boom" has made the rich richer and has lifted no one out of poverty.

These appear to be the rules that are congenial to the highly intelligent people who make them. Moreover, if these are "...the rules that make life more difficult for those people who are trying to navigate everyday life," then total deregulation should work towards ensuring that life gets even more difficult for those forgotten people who must now navigate a leaking ship without a rudder. More and more never seems to be enough for those unfortunate souls whose only purpose and meaning in life is to pursue money and things.

Wisdom has shown us over and over that true happiness and peace of mind can never be bought and sold. While some people think they're living, they may be more dead inside than they even realize. It is obvious that it is far more difficult to navigate everyday life when the lives of everyday people are intentionally made difficult by those whose lives are already easy.

It seems that the double messages that we've been receiving are confounding, and that's probably because they were meant to be. Yet at the same time, they can be influential and persuasive to others. We screen information through our perceptual (intellectual) boundaries. When we see stories of how otherwise intelligent people are so easily duped and swindled, then essentially what we are seeing is the power of perceptual damage. Stories abound of those people -children and adults- who have learned how to mistrust their own perceptions. And of course there are always those who are quick to capitalize on their weaknesses and gullibility.

When this situation occurs it is known as *cognitive dissonance*. Cognitive dissonance is a pattern that occurs more often than we would like to think. Dr. C.E. Weakland and Dr. Paul Watzlavick have shown us that starting in childhood, when a parent says one thing but then does another, then the pattern begins. When a child can see that mom and dad are fighting, but they're told that nothing is wrong, then this begins an inner conflict in the child that cannot be reasoned away by the child.

Another different example is when a child is told that they are loved, but only if they do something for the parent, or act in a certain way. The love that is given conditionally is confusing. If I'm being told that what I'm seeing is not what I'm seeing; that it's up when it's down, or black when it's white, then I am learning to distrust my own sense of reality. We know that later in life this often makes people vulnerable and even gullible. When adults don't trust their own perceptions, they often become vulnerable to gurus, gangs, zealots and demagogues. Persuasive and charismatic individuals are often projected upon with damaging results to the projector. It is always wise, even in the face of persuasive-sounding information, to be cautious of those who insist that they know what's best for us.

It also appears that those who are burdened with a higher IQ should consider that we are all social beings, and as such, we may even have a moral obligation and a social responsibility to help our fellow travelers. Is the value of an education to only do well for ourselves? Sometimes we make life more complicated than it is. And some theories look good on paper but prove much more difficult to implement in reality. Some of the best sounding theories are laid to waste at the foot of something else that is proven to be more pragmatic and effective. People who don't trust themselves become easy victims of others' ideas. It remains vitally important for us to make decisions, not only based on our minds, but also on the voice within.

The authors' policy prescription for the criminal justice system is just to make it simpler. While this certainly carries a grain of truth, it may end up being a task that is difficult to accomplish. Complications that are seldom if ever considered are the very things that have been mentioned in our own text. Along with normalized injustice is the fact that people in powerful positions can easily fall prey to their own preferences, prejudices and foibles. We hear more and more about the cases where innocent people have been wrongly convicted of crimes and serve many years incarcerated for something they didn't do. This doesn't happen to wealthy elitists, who aren't even jailed for the crimes they commit. We also know that in the current atmosphere, more and more positions of power are being filled by those like-minded individuals who serve their sponsors and political supporters, and who also have difficulty maintaining fairness and objectivity.

What's being drained from our communities is a sense of trust in the people that are elected to support us, and in faith in the very cornerstones of our democracy. When judges and other officials are given positions of power based on the special interests of certain groups, how can people possibly believe that fair and impartial decisions will be made? So when we talk about something simpler that could be put into place, let's ensure that the laws apply to everyone equally, in spite of their color or socioeconomic status. Dr. King also said that it is always the right time to do the right thing. This appears to have less to do with having a higher IQ and more to do with having a sense of honesty, fairness, and social justice. The criminal justice system is already simple -if you have no money, you simply get no justice.

As the issues return to a disdain for those of low cognitive ability, wedges are driven further by proposing that people of low intelligence just don't know why marriage is a good thing (p. 544). We could find no graphs or data in support of this allegation. Our first observation is that, quite the contrary, marriage may **not** always be a good thing. They say that life is short, however life can be very long if one chooses the wrong partner. It is patently clear that people of all stripes experience relationship problems, separations and even divorce at some point in their lives. To suggest that it is only those of low IQ who experience these difficulties **because** they are less intelligent, is simply not true.

Accomplished researchers, who expend so many resources attempting to prove that human beings are less than them, should always be willing to present data that might support **all** their claims. While some degree of intelligence may be helpful in managing our relationships, when we experience loss and rejection, being smart doesn't seem to be that helpful. As many of us have learned, when betrayal, sex and lies, abandonment and rejection enter into the picture, then any semblance of intellect and reason flies out the window. Other pejorative remarks in this section of the book purport that "… less intelligent people are less likely to think through their issues." In matters of the heart, when people fight and argue, we would love to see the research on how often intelligent people stop to put on their thinking caps.

As the plot thickens we seem to be observing more personal and moralistic pronouncements that seem unbecoming to objective scientists. "If you are an unmarried mother, you have no legal basis for demanding that the father of the child provide support." From reviewing the text, we can't be sure when our researchers became legal experts, in that they so freely share their legal advice here. Regardless of the next statement, this one could have been used as an excuse for deadbeat dads who refuse to take responsibility for a situation in which they indeed played a major role. Then, as if personal rancor were taking over we read, "If you are an unmarried father you have no legal standing regarding the child -not even a right to see the child, let alone any basis honored by society for claiming he or she is yours." Without knowing the surrounding circumstances, we would have a tendency to allow experts, the parents and the courts to make the determinations in these matters. Since when are researchers allowed to declare what rights anyone has? We do know that from a clinical standpoint, scolding and shaming people is simply not an effective means by which to create meaningful change. Again, we simply suggest that this diatribe is unfitting to any objective scientist with a degree of equanimity. To position oneself as the representative of all of society is also quite a stretch.

Furthermore, framing the sexual revolution (which could encompass the current women's movement) as the culprit for any failings of the institution of marriage is absurd. This in itself is misogynistic and only demonstrates the ignorance and total misunderstanding of the masculine and feminine dynamic. This is the imbalance in our society which in turn is a reflection of the imbalance **in ourselves**. We propose that it is precisely the abuse and mistreatment of women, by men, that has been a catalyst for a needed change. When anyone takes a stand against injustice, this is known as justifiable anger, and it shouldn't be framed as untoward behavior. This is not about men versus women, it is more about an inner balance of the masculine and the feminine. This can prove to be difficult in that it isn't so much about changing things on the outside. While it is of great importance to fight for the changes that need to occur in society, the changes that are the most vital are those that we make on the inside.

The idea that it is the culture itself begging for change needs to be accompanied by the reality that the culture is composed of the collective, and the collective is comprised of individuals. So any real change will begin in the individual. When young children are taught that they may be special, then they can easily adopt the idea that they deserve special privileges and are more important than other people. This then begins to intellectually separate them from the collective. When children are spoiled and given everything they desire, it is easy to see how this can begin to form a personality that is prone to narcissism, megalomania, grandiosity and a sense of entitlement. There is clearly a balance between discipline and permissiveness.

Antisocial behavior can appear in many forms, and television and the media thrive on the crime shows and talent searches that contribute to inflation, self-absorption and other disorders of the ego. People aren't informed about just how quickly fame and fortune can vanish. In a culture that engenders self-centeredness and vanity, people don't learn that stardom and heroism can be short-lived, or that the beauty of youth fades in time as the laws of nature take their course. The irony here is that it is the anti-aging hype (ageism) and trying to stay young forever that are exactly the **unnatural** and unrealistic approaches to life. Whatever one might choose to believe -just try not getting old! It may be wiser to face the inevitable with dignity and integrity instead of swimming upstream. And yet fortunes will continue to be made by people who capitalize on everything, and shamelessly convince others that they are not acceptable for who they are and what they look like.

So if we're wise, then we learn to remain vigilant of the opposing elements in our lives, so that the pendulum doesn't swing too far in either direction. There is of course a middle path between liking yourself too much and not liking yourself enough. Without reservation, we submit that this is part of the balance that many may seek but few will find. While this does require help from our conscious intellect, this psychological balancing act may only come about with cooperation and interaction from the conscious mind in concert with the unconscious. This will require a major paradigm shift in our thinking and in our culture, and the question is: "Are we really up to the task?"

Returning to the authors' ongoing concerns with relationships and the institution of marriage, we can detect a personal moral imperative that has the tendency to condemn all those who do not choose to marry for whatever reasons. What was said in an earlier segment bears repeating. If the institution of marriage overall is perceived as failing, then it seems clear that this is not the blame of individuals who do not choose to marry. A sound psychological principle that applies here is that no one is ever responsible for our happiness, and we are never responsible for theirs. A state sanctioned union cannot ensure longevity, no matter the vows that are spoken.

At the root of failed relationships and the nuptial dilemma is the attempt to impose our archaic ideas of relatedness onto others regardless of the consequences. The simple fact of the matter is that some couples are meant to be together while others are not. And either way, most couples are going to have to work at it. Alluding to our earlier conversation about the Western phenomenon of romantic love, some marriages are based on what has been described as a form of temporary insanity, whereby decisions to make lifetime commitments are made on the feelings of the moment. Some of those relationships may last and may well involve some degree of love, or they may result in conflict and separation. These are things that hopeless romantics find difficult to hear. These outdated ideas of romantic love are so deeply ingrained that some people become extremely upset when they are told that no one else can really make them happy and whole. They refuse to hear that their happiness is **their** job.

What is not being discussed is that the more popular ideas of romantic love have led to lifetimes of unfulfilled expectations and broken dreams. The next big question we pose is, "Can we afford to continue on this often delusory path that costs us emotionally, physically and monetarily? Sounding paradoxical, we also state that we most assuredly believe in love. And while we feel that it is up to the individual, the next question is, "Just what kind of love would that be?" Many different cultures believe in several different types of *love*, and even have different names for the concept. In America we seem to have only one. And yet we love our parents differently than we love our partners, and we probably love our siblings different than we love our pets. It is not our place to define what love is for others, but from what we've learned, lasting human relationships seem to be more about openness, honesty, communication, loyalty -and last but certainly not least- friendship.

The continuing (unscientific) obsessions with shaming and blaming single, unwed and disadvantaged women, overlooks the history of patriarchal societies that have always ignored, devalued and mistreated women since time immemorial. Without dealing with misogyny's deep roots in the human psyche, then men and even women, will be dragged back down into the mire of bigotry and inequality. While social unrest and protest are important, we continue to overlook what's at the heart of the matter.

As the intellectual assault continues, so do we. The writers of the Bell Curve now suggest that being committed to someone is not the same thing as marriage. Without providing us with their definition of commitment, the inference here of course is that being **officially** committed is a better and a more acceptable arrangement. Technically there is an obvious difference, although we still haven't been told how a court document can keep two people together, never mind that love may not be part of the equation at all. Interestingly, neither love nor the relatedness between two people have ever entered into the authors' discussion of marriage. And a piece of paper does not guarantee a happy, healthy, loving relationship after the ceremony is over.

Couples often come together and grow apart for a variety of reasons and it is not the place of researchers, scientists or psychologists, no matter their clout, to dictate under what circumstances people should marry. Their next fiat might be about how and when couples should argue or when they should part. Being harsh and punitive with women simply because they are single or unwed sounds more like a personal, moralistic view that has little to do with valid scientific research, and even less to do with a genuine concern for healthy, functioning relationships.

Men who have no sense of internal balance see women as weak and inferior, and they experience a great deal of frustration and discomfort around confident and independent women. This becomes important as we watch the current administration pull the plug on the environmental laws that were put in place to protect and save our planet. It is of significance psychologically, because in mythology, nature has always symbolized the feminine and women (Mother Earth -our first mother). Based on the skepticism of these unorthodox ideas, it is not surprising that our continuous mistreatment of women coincides with the equally poor treatment of our earth. We also know that there seems to be a connection with those cultures that exhibit misogynistic tendencies, and those places where war and violence are most likely to occur.

There appears to be no significant evidence to suggest that the decline of the institution of marriage is due to lower cognitive ability. In their own words the authors write, "And yet marriage is still alive and well in the sense that it remains a hugely popular institution." (p. 169)

Professor Campbell tells a story that may be fitting here, as it is a metaphor for our apathy towards nature. A young native boy, who often ventured from his village into the forest, finds a bird with the most beautiful song. Finding the bird's song special, he takes the bird back to his village and begins to feed and nurture the gift that nature has given him. His father is a stoic and practical man, and though he is a good father, he refuses to feed "just" a bird. One day the boy comes home only to find that the unfed bird has died. And as the story goes, when his father killed the bird he killed the song, and when he killed the song, he killed himself.

We will return to statements made earlier in the book because they are relevant to the topics that the authors continue to bring up in these later segments. In addition to the conclusions they've made above, there are other statements that continue to pop up that seem to contradict the assertions made earlier in the text, e.g. "Our impressions of the state of the American family are not necessarily accurate." It would be hard to interpret this in any other way besides the way in which it is stated.

In support of their ideas in this section is yet another chart that we revisit labeled, *"Which Whites Get Married When."* Apparently, using only white subjects and a smaller number of their sample population, the researchers concluded that "IQ has no significant independent role on marriage." Adding to all the confusion, on the following page their graph indicates that within this group, high IQ raises the probability of marriage, obviously only for a select group of white students. This is all preceded by a graph depicting divorce trends from 1920 through 1990 and the actual cause of this naturally occurring trend, all things relevant, has not been established.

Not being researchers or statisticians, these nebulous "facts" seem unclear and can only be confusing to any layperson as well. We're also not clear about just why "smarter people marry less often on a whim," as is suggested. In conjunction with our earlier discussion on projections and compulsive decisions, we cannot presume to know exactly how and why people come together, we can only hypothesize. We don't believe that statistics alone can reveal exactly why people get divorced, whether it be sooner or later. Other than these studies, it seems like only conjecture when we presume that the reason all couples marry or divorce is primarily due to their intelligence.

Confined to the same smaller group of white couples, we've located another chart (p. 174) that provides a percentage of divorce within the first five years of marriage and it is based on I.Q. It is hard to make conclusions based on these relatively small numbers, especially when no minorities or people of color are represented in some of these studies. These particular findings are based on the exclusion of many other people who also marry and live among us. We appear to be living in a multiracial, multicultural society in which many argue that pluralism is realistic and socially beneficial. Consequently, decisions about marriage, divorce, relationships etc. will also vary. If being pluralistic means having multiple parts or features, then even various aspects of intelligence may not be so easy to define or categorize.

We are assured on page 174 that, I.Q. being equal, "children of higher status families were more likely to get divorced than children of lower status families." So again, just having wealth must not a happy home make. When we hear that it is those of higher socioeconomic status that are more likely to divorce, it seems to contradict what we've read before about the superiority of the chosen elites. A little earlier we pointed out that the wealthy and the brightest have become synonymous for the authors. This confluence of the smart and the rich actually begins in part 1 (pp. 25-27), where the cognitive elite are framed as a new emerging class, then continues with suggestive remarks throughout. On page 515 we read: "… the universe of affluent people has become more densely populated with the very bright." This is followed by the matter-of-fact statement that, "Not surprisingly, the interests of affluence and the cognitive elite have begun to blend."

Wealth, having been associated to higher intelligence, then it may be safe to assume that neither privilege nor intelligence are predictors of stability or longevity in the institution of marriage -our original argument. That said, then the wealthy and the more intelligent are no more immune from the scourge of divorce and being single than their "inferior" counterparts, whether they blend together or not.

Staying with the final chapter, we find another example of selective hermeneutics and the argument for prosperity that arises when people attempt to justify their own lust for money and power. It is easy for some to rationalize their desires in order to feel better about themselves, and about things that might not be seen as positive or even ethical. On page 547 the authors of the book lament that "most people quit believing that a person's income on earth reflects God's judgment of his worth..." We're unsure where God talks specifically about proper income distribution in the Bible, but we know that this quote by the authors is somewhat misleading. Along with rugged individualism, this was a belief held primarily by early Puritans, as well as the idea that, "… they all had the duty of working for the greater glory of God." As the adept sociologist, Ian Robertson points out (regarding Puritans): "In their anxiety to find out if they were to be saved, they took signs of success in work as an indication of God's favor..." Again, these are their beliefs, with no expressed desire by God for them to increase their income and wealth, or that he would personally judge their worth on that basis. These beliefs did however, motivate them to work even harder and so they lived in abundance. Moreover, they were forbidden by the Puritan ethic to spend the additional income on luxurious living. (Robertson, 1987)

Something that might also be considered as the big question here, is how anyone can claim to know what God actually said or meant? Religious scholars now speak openly about how Jesus himself never left a written word and that many biblical stories are second and even third hand accounts. Some modern scholars have even pointed out that Jesus spoke in symbols, and that the confusion lies in attempting to understand most of these stories literally. At one point in the Bible, Jesus declares, "I speak in symbols but you do not understand." The above statements suggest that God attaches the measure of a human being to how much money they have, although this isn't the God or the Christian morals that most of us learned about.

In fact, many different religions and their differing versions of the bible are the result of certain groups that could not come to agreement about what Jesus said or what he may have meant. The above statement seems to favor the privileged and yet Jesus spoke of how difficult it was for a rich man to enter the kingdom of heaven, in metaphor. What their selected passage also suggests is that consequently, the poor and the indigent are in disfavor, but this doesn't seem to square with the passage from Matthew that was quoted earlier (Matt: 25: 35-36) regarding caring for the poor and the least among us. We also know that scholars are actually unclear about who wrote what in the Bible, since we now know that there was an array of contributors. The authors' stance appears to conflict with the man of love and peace to whom they refer.

Selecting certain passages to interpret a certain way can mean that it is easy to manipulate biblical interpretations and to overlook those passages in scripture that do not suit our needs, while emphasizing the ones that serve our purpose. And again, Shakespeare was correct, "The devil *can* cite scripture to his own purpose" (italics mine). Even more disturbing are those who attempt to normalize avarice while ignoring and even condemning, poverty and deprivation. The New Testament personifies wealth and greed as a false god, often referring to material wealth as *mammon*. It seems clear that the new gods of Profit and Gain would have been considered as an evil influence in our modern world. Maybe it is time to follow Jesus' example and chase the money-changers from the temple. And it would be interesting to see how staunch believers would interpret the aforementioned passage by Luke 16:13, "You cannot serve both God and money." It is sad to watch so many who have so much material success have so little inner peace, in spite of their beliefs.

We believe that it is both relevant and vital to discuss the issues that continue to have a major impact on our world and how we live in it. As mentioned earlier, even our college campuses are contaminated by the subjective values and standards embraced in volumes like The Bell Curve. Somewhere it was said that human beings believe just as they breathe -in order to survive; that faith is an instinctive response to aspects of our existence -an existence that no one can fully or truly explain.

Where We Are Truly Headed

We must never lose sight of the fact that the ideas within the volume we are observing had a major impact on the strict laws and policies that have only grown increasingly harsher as we rapidly approach the year 2020. As the veil is lifted, the championing of social engineering and an attitude of disdain and disregard for the least among us become more and more obvious, and more and more dangerous. To avoid and circumvent women's rights and issues of poverty is neither prudent nor realistic, for we are only as strong as our weakest link.

While the surviving author of this text attempts to revive the ideology that only serves elitism and plutocracy, the stark reality of shrinking choices and opportunities for those who don't make the mark continues. In an overpopulated world, the destruction of a woman's right to choose what to do with her own body is no longer just a personal issue -it may even be a more pragmatic issue about our own survival. Imposing our own values on others with a political sledgehammer has less to do about respecting life, and more to do with power, control and a self-righteous mindset.

The pro-life stance ignores people's rights in order to impose their personal morals onto others. If the government were to order all good Christian families to sacrifice their first born, as a place in the Bible suggests, would those moral zealots then willingly do what they were told? When I attempt to impose my values and beliefs onto others, I must fully understand that this is more about something unsettling that is going on inside of **me**. If it means that I hate or harm anyone then **I** alone am responsible for my animosity and my lack of self-knowledge, self-awareness and self-control.

Intransigent pro-life advocates overlook the fact that, subsequent to their birth, these children are then denied adequate sustenance and a good education. The draconian laws enacted by the few will now forget, avoid and deny any future responsibility to those same children whose birth they championed. To an independent mind, this might be suggestive of a stance that is more pro-birth than pro-life.

The attitudes and opinions presented in the book we're observing are echoed in the rhetoric of the current administration. We've also learned that the mantra *America First* was a political strategy used by other leaders in the past. Its origins are rooted in a similar populist movement that first reared its ugly head during the 20's and 30's. It is quite interesting to note that the literal definition of *populism* is, "A political philosophy supporting the rights and power of the people in their struggle against the privileged elite." Already discussed, these movements usually begin with uncertainty and economic downturns. As mentioned, power grabs begin with scapegoating, vitriol, demagoguery and divisiveness. Having discussed the psychological aspects, we now understand that this more modern version of populism is about oppressive, fearful elites who are ever so ready to lower the lance and attack others for their own inner shortcomings. However, the language of returning to some pretentious past is pure fantasy and it is a facade used to romanticize a dangerous and regressive agenda.

Make America Great Again was a ploy used by others and while sounding patriotic, is delusional but effective. Returning to the past is no more feasible than it is to return home after we grow up. If we do happen to go back to live in our home of origin, the atmosphere is usually toxic or unhealthy. When used politically, these nostalgic notions arouse feelings that are appealing to those who have not gained their personal and emotional autonomy. And yet in America, it is not unusual to hear the stories about grown up children in their 20's and 30's living in their parents' basement.

The word *nostalgia* has as its original meaning, "a yearning for home." But poetry and even modern pop lyrics have suggested that we can never go home again. In the world of therapy, it is known that the true sign of maturity and independence is when one is able to break away from the parents physically **and** psychologically. This in no way disrespects our parents, but rather, it is a psychological reality that needs to occur in order for us to truly grow up. For some adults, it may be time to sever the umbilical cord. And if any of these ideas become upsetting or troubling in any way, may we brazenly suggest that people look within.

Another connection that has been made returns us to a primary myth in the Bible. If, as suggested by modern religious scholars, these ancient stories could be seen in symbolic fashion, then their treasure trove of meaning could be unlocked and a new era of understanding could begin. The story of the Garden of Eden can be a valuable lesson when seen on a deeper level, and it teaches us that we can't go home. Without going into detail, when Adam and Eve are evicted from the garden something interesting occurs. Symbolically, paradise itself can be seen as that place of tranquility and oneness where the couple has no problems and feels no pain. Upon committing the act of attempting to gain knowledge (eating the forbidden fruit) they are expelled from the garden into a life of pain and suffering. There are many other elements in the story that have been deciphered, but for our purposes, a physical attempt at returning to our place of origin is not an option. Literal interpretations have made many of these valuable stories and myths difficult to apprehend and everyone is left to choose for themselves.

Some psychological interpretations liken the state of paradise to the safe sanctuary of the uterus, where we are held safely in the womb of our mothers. When infants come into the world of pain and pleasure they usually enter crying. Thus begins the first separation and there is no turning back.

Some people have even interpreted the use of alcohol (and some drugs) as symbolically attempting to return to that initial comfort and security. In the Bible, that return is totally discouraged by two cherubim with flaming swords at the heavenly gates that would deny us any re-entrance.

Whatever one chooses to believe, these stories have sustained people since time immemorial. They continue to have resonance because of the powerful pull and the symbolic meaning that they carry for people in so many different places and cultures. For us, moving from paradise and thus forfeiting that original place of bliss and perfection, is the more honest and realistic state of being. And though it may be filled with pain and suffering, to face our fears and become more conscious makes us more real and more whole human beings. It is only in death that we will feel no pain. Most people will go to great lengths to avoid the emotional pain that is inherent to life; in doing so they also avoid the inevitable appointment with their deeper selves.

The other focus of attention by the authors continues to be on immigration in this country, and having addressed that issue as well, we would only add that there are other voices that have indicated that our economy is based in part on the labor of those people who perform the servile work that most Americans decline doing. In a recent interview with Apple C.E.O. Tim Cook, he stated that immigrants would be needed to resupply this country with a workforce that is receding. He also asserted that rather than being a drain on our economy, they will actually increase our GDP.

In finishing our observations of *A Place for Everyone*, we concur with the authors notion that peoples' lives are not equal. People are more often judged and treated by what they have and what they look like, rather than what Dr. King referred to as "the content of their character." This might be a stretch for those who prefer to measure peoples' value by a few standard deviation points.

In classic demagogic style politicians and ideologues continuously convey the message that they are the sole representatives of the truth and the good by shamelessly attacking the truth and the good.

In reality, people are not equal -not the same- and perhaps this is also for the better. It would be a boring, stagnant world if everyone looked the same and believed in the same things. By the same token, people shouldn't be relegated to a life of scorn and deprivation because they are different.

Max Weber, the acclaimed sociologist, was said to have had a stronger influence on sociology than any other single individual. In his discourse, *On Law in Economy and Society* (1967) we read: "The fates of human beings are not equal. Men differ in their state of health and wealth or social status or what not. Simple observations show that in every such situation he who is more favored feels the never ceasing need to look upon his position as in some way 'legitimate,' and upon his advantage being 'deserved' and the other's disadvantage as being brought on by the latter's 'fault.' That the purely accidental causes of the difference may be ever so obvious makes no difference to some."

We would only add that this important social scientist could not have foreseen the avalanche of disparity and division that would follow his observations. He could not have known that the advantages he spoke of would no longer just be accidental, but would become the obsession of those who would readily sell their souls for those advantages. Applying the firm belief in his concept of *value-freedom* to responsible professionals, this realistic but unrealized standard supports the **absence** of personal values and bias in **all** professional work.

The conclusion of *A Place for Everyone* is unsurprisingly predictable and much like the rest of the text. This segment is a somewhat confusing admixture of ideas, and without the usual downpour of data and statistics, that were clearly crafted to convince us about the inferiority of the weakest and most vulnerable members of our society. These ideas are the sine qua non of the text and its primary message. As it makes an attempt at presenting opinionated answers to vital issues, it wastes no time in denigrating and denouncing its targeted scapegoats, hidden behind a veil of scientific research. We can only conclude that the "place for everyone" that the authors hint at is only for everyone who thinks, acts and looks like us (i.e. them). Their final remarks are also predicated on research that leads back to their original intentions -to prove that there are some people in our society that are unworthy, and simply less than the rest of us. Their diligent research was successfully refuted by several reputable scientists, however it is hard to douse a fire that is fueled by ego inflation and the inability to change.

The second paragraph of their conclusion clearly brings to light their baleful intentions. The next attack on the poor and the unwanted, who are not endowed with **their** superior intellects: "We have tried to point out what a small segment of the population accounts for such a large proportion of those problems. To the extent that the problems of this small segment are susceptible to social engineering solutions at all, they should be highly targeted" (pp. 549-550). So, the "…small segment of the population" that is the cause of all America's problems should be "targeted." These are the "expendable masses" that Nietzsche spoke of, that now need to be targeted, set upon, and even eliminated to appease the arrogant, dispassionate elite. This also creates spurious reasoning for why these chosen people should **not** pay their taxes. This appears to be their intellectual answer to the poverty, inequality, deprivation and social injustice that these highly regarded "scientists" aspired to. Interestingly enough, Murray has bristled at any suggestion that his writing could even be considered as racist, eugenic or biased. This, as he callously uses the term "social engineering solutions."

The following "solutions" to the nation's problems followed with their ideas of improving education, but only "for those who have the greatest potential." We can assume that only savant elitists would be qualified enough to make those determinations. Using euphemistic language and vague assertions in *answer 4*, readers are encouraged to "a return to individualism." Individualism was a term that has already been described as the outdated puritanical value, *rugged individualism.* The study of etymology teaches us that some words (and terms) change over time taking on new connotations and different meanings. *Individualism* is a term that was a major value of industrial societies, later becoming more emphasized in our postindustrial society. Sadly, it is now used to fuel modern divisive thinking.

The growing problem with modern individualism is that the people who live in these societies are increasingly concerned with their own self-fulfillment. Again, this is a self-serving mindset where individual needs and desires become more important than social and traditional obligations. In its very nature it creates a separatist "what's in it for me" attitude. There is then no concern for others and no desire to work towards the common goals that might actually improve society and culture. It has facilitated a social dilemma that is damaging to both society and the individual. It turns united states into divided states, with deleterious effects. In our society, it is also considered as a manifestation of the psychological split that resides in the individual psyches of an increasingly neurotic culture. Originally, the word *neurosis* meant "split."

After generalizing about these certain groups (i.e. women, minorities and the impoverished) with obvious disdain, and garnering support for the exclusion of those targeted groups from fair and equal policy changes, we are then bewildered by the next statement: "A person should not be judged as a member of a group but as an individual." Individuals are what make up a group. Regressing backward to individualism, which is not a doctrine, is also not the same thing as judging someone as an individual, however all these muddled concepts are described as a foundation of the American doctrine: "With the cornerstone of the American doctrine in place, group differences can take their appropriately insignificant place in affecting American life." At this point, readers are allowed to make their own determinations, however, what comes to mind here is an old expression by another mistreated and unwanted group, the American Indians: "Paleface speaks with forked tongue."

We contend that narcissism, avarice, megalomania, and other serious disorders are the direct consequences of ego inflation and being overly concerned about one's own needs and desires. While it is important to be one's self, it is of equal importance to know who that is. We are social animals by nature, and as such, we must relate to each other in a healthier way. Decadence, anomie and self-centeredness were precisely what noted sociologist Emile Durkheim warned us about in the late 19th century and it seems to be an integral part of the *New World Order* that's been planned for us.

Durkheim theorized about the final results of the division of labor with its emphasis on differences and individuality. He believed that the condition of anomie could set in, which is a state of isolation and confusion in both the society and the individual. When social norms are absent, weak or conflicting then anomie spreads and people begin to feel more and more detached from each other (and now we are aided by the impersonal social media). He noted that traditional societies were held together by a social cohesion that was based on the similarity of its members. The lack of commitment to shared norms and the breakdown of social guidelines for personal conduct, he predicted, would move people to pursue their own private interests with no regard for the interests of society as a whole. He realized that this would render the social control of individuals ineffective. He concluded that increased specialization has two major (and related) effects: it changes the very nature of the bonds that hold a society together, and it encourages individualism at the expense of the community. He believed that the dangerous social consequences of all this could even result in disintegration (Robertson, 1987). This appears to have been a 19th century blueprint for what is now occurring.

In their closing chapter we note the self-adulation regarding America being "one of the friendliest, most eager to oblige, neighborly peoples in the world." This statement is not supported in the text, or by the current climate, where children are being separated from their parents and imprisoned. While many Americans still believe in taking in the huddled masses, others may have forgotten that their ancestors were themselves most likely immigrants that came here to find a better life. Having quoted Tocqueville earlier, we find one more observation to be appropriate for many people at this time, when he said, "They call it the American dream because you have to be asleep to believe it."

It remains important to point out that it was their own prejudicial remarks and downgrading conclusions that may have played a part in making the Bell Curve such a popular firestorm. The authors stated that "Cognitive partitioning will continue…," which may have been more of a desire that planned for the future of those they chose to separate from. They also iterate some vague notions about weaving safety nets (which they don't believe in) for the disadvantaged, "…so that their mistakes and misfortunes are mitigated and withstood with a little help from their friends." In other words, since poverty and deprivation are entirely their doing, the poor deserve no help and they might be able to survive by obtaining charity, "with a little help from their friends," which is probably not what the Beatles had in mind either.

The remaining paragraph continues with a separatist, elitist ideal, while ignoring any collective **or** governmental responsibility towards our neediest neighbors. Not slowing down, on page 551, we find a direct plea to "those who are smart enough and rich enough." They are simply encouraged to "...exploit the complex rules to their advantage, and buy their way out of the social institutions that no longer function..." First of all, they've created the rules that they say no longer function, and now they are prompted to take advantage of their own rules and institutions even further. Essentially, this callous attitude and denial of any responsibility will allow them to live unimpeded by pesky and "unfair" taxes (and laws) that support the entire social structure; the same taxes that everyone else are just expected to pay.

Their dark, self-serving dreams and plans are coming to fruition. The social apathy, cheating, mendacity and tax evasion that were supported and encouraged resulted in all their legitimized scams and would deny this country billions of dollars in revenues. Shirking their patriotic responsibilities, until the patriotic fever suits their needs, the affluent and their chosen leaders are successfully bringing the rest of "undeserving" America to its knees. And they hide behind the flag and the bible to maintain power and their obscene wealth. They simply do not understand that you cannot buy three of the most important things in life: true love, real friendships and peace of mind.

To further state their case, and again, appealing to their wealthier readers "...so heavily concentrated among those who fit that description..." they encourage the smartest and the richest to "recognize the ways in which public policy has come to deny those goods to those who are not smart enough and rich enough." This double-talk would suggest that, contrary to everything we've read, maybe these superior beings should at least be aware of the harmful laws and policies that **they** have helped to create. And what good does it do to recognize a serious situation if you have no intentions of helping to remedy it?

The dire need to control others is a psychological deficit (discussed on page 94) and it is nothing new, however it is obvious that some would love to live in the past, and then fight to stay stuck. If the so-called cognitive elite were truly secure in their belief system, their faith and their knowledge base, then it's clear that they would have no need to go out of their way to suppress the information that they do not agree with. And they certainly wouldn't feel the need to kill and oppress others to prove they were right. Propaganda, distorted thinking, proselytization and the re-framing of vital issues, only serves wealthy elitists who use subservient sycophants as pawns in their nefarious game. So afraid and insecure are they in their long-held beliefs and their cherished values that the *thought police* spend an inordinate amount of time, money and energy to suppress ideas and information.

This is misoneism plain and simple, and has its basis in primitive thinking, and group think doesn't bode well for any kind of peaceful or progressive future. Convincing those, already incapable of critical, independent thinking, is what Jung was alluding to when he used the terms "mass man" and "herd mentality."

The time has come to be frank. Caught in a web of deceit and confusion, and after all the previous pejorative remarks and conclusions, we can only wonder how a truly intelligent, critical thinker could perceive this text as innocent, straightforward or honest. A proponent of convoluted logic might perceive these findings as tempting, however we return to our earlier premise that people are drawn to the ideas that fit their personalities and who they already are. To see past the statistical morass into what is lurking below does not actually require being in the top decile on a graph or a chart. While this may be unpalatable to some, it can also be the catalyst that calls the rest of us, who actually care about each other, to search our own souls.

Having remained true to their cause throughout the text, we now find the last sentences of the last chapter quite remarkable. With an odd and fleeting sense of compassion, we hear the authors assert that, "At the heart of our thought is the quest for human dignity." At long last, we are told that the most precious reward that we can confer upon each other "is a place as a valued fellow citizen." These are nice-sounding sentiments, however we are more inclined to believe that we are brought together by our common humanity, and respecting each other as human beings is more aligned with the writings of our predominant system of faith and the founding fathers. Many people understand that we are a nation of immigrants and maybe we could begin by respecting cultural diversity, as well as the feminine. This can only occur when we have a deeper understanding of ourselves, and we find our own humanity.

On Human Dignity

The end of the final chapter affords us the opportunity to discuss the term *dignity*, which the authors have told us "...is the central measure of success...for this government is to permit people to live lives of dignity -not to give them dignity..." (p. 551). We have found no clear evidence that Americans feel that it is government's responsibility to render dignity to anyone. In fact, some of our politicians and their policies would belie the notion that this actually occurs. The callous and punitive attitude towards the refugees fleeing oppression and violence now and in the past, confirms that this was never our goal. The psychological damage that's been done to a multitude of children speaks to a total lack of concern for the dignity of anyone.

We would also posit the notion that dignity is not given. Honor and dignity are the gifts that people give to themselves. Yet even this is too simplistic. As social creatures we live in a society with other social beings, along with all the laws and mores that accompany those situations. We could also easily assume that freedom and equality are closely associated to dignity, in that without them, dignity itself is difficult to maintain. And if freedom, equality and justice are not facilitated by government in this society, then who will defend or uphold our Constitution, or the Declaration of Independence? Former conservative U.S. leader, G.W. Bush openly declared that the Constitution was "… just a goddamned piece paper." It seems much easier for those of privilege, who've never experienced hunger, disparity or deprivation to **talk** about freedom, justice and dignity, but it is truly the rhetoric of failure.

When it becomes easy to read outlandish and self-contradictory remarks like, "It is time for Americans once again to try living with inequality…," then America as a country, and we as Americans, have truly lost our way. More fair-minded and intelligent readers can't even relate to this regressive statement. And history might prove that we have never really lived in this country without some level of disparity. This creative use of language only appeals to those who would like to confirm what they already think. Maybe this is what Lincoln tried to impart during his first inaugural address when he was forced to call for the majority rule to be balanced by constitutional restraints, appealing to "the better angels of our nature."

Under the rubric of ego inflation fall the darker angels of greed, arrogance and mean-spiritedness, which have become normalized in our culture. We reemphasize that ego inflation is the disease of our day. We navigate in dangerous waters when a spurious sense of entitlement, which is elitism, and intellectualism, which rationalizes our bad behavior, are conflated. Some of the most intelligent and well-intentioned people in the world operate unconsciously at times, and when their actions are not tempered by compassion and sensitivity, then we have what we are now facing. It is remarkable how some people can so easily inflict pain and suffering upon others, however, it's easy to hurt others when you don't feel pain.

If the basic definition of dignity is our idea of our own inherent worth and nobility, then that self-worth is connected to what we value and how others might value us. One of the most significant and influential attempts at identifying the core values that most Americans share were the ideas outlined by the sociologist, Robin Williams in 1970 (Robertson, 1987). Among the fifteen basic orientation values that America espouses, and he outlined, we point to only six elements that we felt were the most relevant to our discussion:

Proposition 4. Humanitarianism: "Americans regard themselves as kindly charitable people always ready to come to the aid of the less fortunate."

It seems clear that the adverb Williams uses here is "always."

Proposition 8. Equality: "Americans claim to believe in human equality, particularly in equality of opportunity; they generally relate to one another in an informal <u>egalitarian</u> way." (underlining mine)

Authors of the Bell Curve not only rebuke egalitarianism, but would readily deny targeted groups of people equal political, economic, and social opportunities. They would also deny basic civil rights under the laws of the state and under the norms of human decency.

Proposition 9. Freedom: "The freedom of the individual is regarded as one of the most important values in American life; Americans believe devoutly they are and should remain free."

We note here that freedom should be defined in the context in which it is being used. If freedom actually is an important value to Americans, then they must clearly understand that the freedom of everyone, not just the disadvantaged, is now under siege more than at any other time in our history. "None are more hopelessly enslaved than those who falsely believe they are free." -Goethe

Proposition 10. External Conformity: "Despite their expressed belief in "rugged individualism" Americans <u>tend to be conformists</u> and are suspicious of others who are not." (underlining mine)

This conformity and compliance can quickly become dangerous behavior when it is unconscious and experienced on a collective level. This sort of herd mentality was briefly discussed earlier in our text, and when collectively taken to extremes, was aptly described as unconscious behavior by Levy-Bruhl. In fact, people have been attacked, tortured, banished and even killed when attempting to think for themselves or go their own way. We've already talked about man's journey beginning in groups, which was necessary for his survival. In our modern era, we've gone to extremes with the ideas of individualism, tribalism and a self-serving agenda that now separate us from each other. Again, the desired goal is balance and harmony.

At this point in our discussion we feel the need to digress. We would like to interject with a metaphor that might better demonstrate the gravity of the situation. Sometimes, when people are not able to break free from the limits and boundaries that are imposed by others, it can have devastating effects.

The ancient Marabout of North Africa provide us with a profound story that is a symbolic representation of the self-limiting and self-defeating cycle that often has serious consequences:

First, a tribal member draws a circle in the sand using a simple stick. The circle can be thought of as representing the world. Then a live scorpion (symbolizing man) is placed in the center of the circle. Onlookers watch intensely while the animal scurries about within the limits of the circle that was drawn. Next, the stick is used to draw a straight line that dissects the circle into halves. The scorpion remains in one half of the circle, frantically moving about, but never crossing the "imaginary" lines drawn for it. At last, a small area just big enough for its body is drawn. The scorpion then spins around and around in a frenzy, never daring to move beyond its limited boundaries. Finally, in a state of chaos and confusion, the creature stings itself to death.

Proposition 13. Democracy: "Americans regard their form of government as highly democratic, and believe that every citizen should have the right of political participation."

As mentioned, plutocrats and their elitist think tanks, have proven to be instrumental in utilizing underhanded political tactics that always give them an advantage. Stacking the federal courts and the Supreme Court, suppressing our rights to vote, along with other surreptitious measures, undermines the very fabric of democracy and freedom by those who are driven to have power and control over others.

Proposition 15. Group Superiority Themes: "A strong counter-value to that of individual personality is the one that places a higher value on some racial, ethnic, class or religious groups than others."

We believe that this definitely has more to do with who is defining those values and who wields the most power, and therefore, has the loudest voice. Following the premise that the powerful and the affluent are gaining more and more wealth and power, then it is only logical to conclude that their major influence over politics, economics, law, and the media, routinely tips the scale in their favor. The higher values at this point in time seem to be control, wealth, militarism, white nationalism and of course fascism.

Whether examined individually or together, these established core American values clearly seem to contradict the ideas that are postulated in the Bell Curve, in spite of its plethora of graphs and statistics. People are left to draw their own conclusions, however the denigration and oppression of women, minorities and other unfortunate souls that live among us appear to be anything but American. It is also in stark contrast to the words of the Founders and the basic teachings of the Christian Church.

There is a divergence of understanding when it comes to our ideas about human nature, and we make no attempt to fully define or unravel its mystery here. We must however be mindful of those who would manipulate the language and information that can deeply affect our thinking and behavior, and our own human nature. And while semantics are important, the key may lie in knowing and trusting ourselves.

Most people might agree with a statement like, "Human nature, being what it is, there will always be wars and conflict." While this seems like a logical and reasonable assertion, it is not completely accurate. War and violence cannot be assumed to always be a fixed part of human nature.

In 1935, an anthropologist named Kilton Stewart traveled to central Malaysia where he studied a tribe called the Senoi Indians. He was amazed when he discovered that these so-called primitives had found no need for wars, jails, police or mental hospitals. In fact, there had not been a reported crime of violence in their community for around 200 years. They actually created a culture that fully believed in their dreams, and they seemed to be in touch with something much deeper inside of themselves.

There are other primitive cultures the world over that do not partake in war. The pygmies of the Ituri Forest in central Africa are not warring people, along with the Lepcha of the Himalayas, the Arapesh of New Guinea, as well as the Shoshone of the western United States. And yet they are the ones that are considered primitive! We can admit to being a violent and aggressive lot, however the leitmotif of the book we are reviewing sings the praises of just how important human intelligence is supposed to be. Just who are the primitive ones?

Primate studies as well have shown us that the complete acceptance of our species as natural killers should be restudied. The chimpanzee was once considered our closest primate ancestor, and they are known to be very aggressive at times. More recently, deep in the African Congo, primates who closely resemble their chimp cousins were rediscovered. Once thought to be extinct, the African Bonobos not only have a matriarchal family structure, but we've learned that they do not attack and kill other primates. In fact, it has been observed that when other primates encroach upon their territory, they actually begin to work in cooperation with their intruders. Through DNA research we've also learned that Bonobo primates are actually more closely related to man than the chimpanzee.

We know that there are other species that can be quite violent and aggressive, however man can easily be thought of as one of the cruelest. Along with the continuing mistreatment of the earth and each other, just how far has our superior cognitive ability brought us? Maybe we could take some lessons from those very creatures and civilizations that we arrogantly view as being so far beneath us.

As Heraclitus noted that everything changes, this would include knowledge and what we think we know. What we think of as factual today could very well be determined as invalid tomorrow. Social scientists all seem to agree that human nature, if there is such a thing, is highly flexible and a product of the interaction between biological potentials and the learning experiences of the particular culture that we happen to live in. Broadly speaking, and depending on our culture, human nature is what we make of it. Having said this, when we allow our instincts to direct our behavior, then intellectualism be damned.

If our actions and behavior promote and perpetuate cruelty, inequity, divisiveness and inhumanity then perhaps it is time that we begin to reassess the meaning of our own human nature. This also supports a more advanced and inclusive notion of being a universal citizen, with the full realization that we are all interconnected, interdependent and interrelated. These profound realizations will rely on the inner work that can only be done by each of us. This then has the ability to make the welcomed, meaningful, and more lasting transformation, that we would all like to see in our world.

In psychological language, the old ego must die (symbolically) before the new one can be born -a personal renaissance. And we can't have a resurrection without a crucifixion. Within the collective however, Hegel also suggested that even a civilization cannot become conscious of itself, it cannot recognize its own significance, until it is so mature that it begins to approach its own death.

At the end of the last chapter the authors state that "the success of each human life is not measured externally, but internally; that of all the rewards that we can confer on each other, the most precious is a place as a valued human being." It is interesting to note that the purpose of our little volume has been to emphasize the first part of this statement. It is clear that there wouldn't have been a need for this book to have been written if the volume in question would not have contradicted the above statement. It seems pretty obvious that from all the charts and statistics to their conclusive remarks, the Bell Curve was clearly meant to measure, label and judge those people who the authors determined were useless and unworthy.

The second half of that closing remark is also an interesting choice of words, for perhaps the most precious thing that we could render to our fellow man includes an opportunity for success and the pursuit of happiness. This might begin with the basic human kindness that actually makes people feel like valued human beings. This is not a gift that the privileged and the cognitively superior graciously bestow upon those who they deem as deserving. This is a basic human right that most people yearn for and every human being deserves.

Elitism, Fascism and Related Topics

The Afterword of the Bell Curve finds its surviving author (Murray) vigorously scrambling to defend he and his colleague's work. This is understandable as it required a considerable amount of time, effort, and generous support from wealthy, conservative supporters. We've already spoken about the uproar that their volume caused and how it may have been their pejorative remarks, prejudicial inferences and condescending conclusions that galvanized their critics.

Even in their concluding remarks they challenged their own audience about white America's discomfort and sensitivity over this country's dark history of slavery. Labeling human sensitivity as "a disorder" only serves to show everyone their own lack of sensitivity. Digging a little deeper into the roots of elitist thinking and right wing propaganda, it is evident that their plans were made decades ago and, now in power, their goals to dismantle democracy and have things their way have been relentless.

After the 60's and 70's saw the downfall of another corrupt and arrogant leader, vast networks of conservative groups and organizations began to pop up like crabgrass in early summer. As mentioned earlier, a newly elected conservative would be installed to escalate foreign intervention and begin an all-out attack on the social welfare programs that were put into place by more kind and generous leaders. In fact, most god-fearing conservatives were outraged by the long-haired protesters that were brazen enough to demand freedom, equality and an end to war. It was even reported that the former Hollywood star (his stardom questionable), Ronald Reagan was not conservative enough for their taste...and the rest is not only history, but it is also our perilous present.

Unhappy about civil unrest, dissension and America's disenchantment with questionable political activities, the conservative party began its takeover decades ago, and with that, its crusade to crush its opponents and establish what was proudly referred to as their *New World Order*. Or, what I've referred to as, *The New Manifest Destiny*.

Angered by Americans' demands for freedom and justice at the time, Lewis Powell (a prominent attorney) would soon be elected to the Supreme Court. Anxious to serve in the interests of the plutocrats, he wrote a letter designed to influence powerful leaders in business and politics entitled, *Attack on American Free Enterprise*, in which he warned wealthy businessmen about the anti-corporate, anti-business, and what he felt was an anti-American attitude that was developing in this country. He may have overlooked the fact that this was also seen as an anti-war, anti-corruption and anti-greed movement that coincided with the debacle of Watergate and the failed war in Southeast Asia, along with the other unethical foreign invasions of the day.

Powell then went on to incite -already voracious- corporate leaders when telling them that they were ignoring a grave crisis, then encouraging them to "… stop suffering in impotent silence, and launch a counterattack," in an effort to persuade the American public of the value of the free enterprise system.

This appealed to the insecurities of business magnates, whose measure of worth always relies on their investments and how much is in their portfolios. Their very character and who they actually are as human beings is never given a second thought.

This call to arms helped to motivate ultra-right conservatives who set in motion the political-intellectual movement that would redirect our democracy. Beginning with elitist thinkers like the beer tycoon, Joseph Coors of the Coors Brewing Company, they've used their wealth and power to build an effective propaganda machine utilizing the mass media, which they had already laid claim to. Members of the Coors family would go on to run for political office; big business and government have been bed-partners for a very long time. In just one example, Coors lost a political election due to his rightist ideas and his own conservative agenda. Promoting ideas like allowing firearms on college campuses, his ideas were predicated on fear and distrust, safety and security, much like the propaganda that drives today's national politics. Elitists refuse to see their endless interventions and occupations as a primary cause of the current global crisis. They deny to the end that it is their own dark behavior that has put the world and nature itself in extreme peril. Over the years, Coors Brewing has faced several charges for polluting the cool, clean mountain streams from where (they boast) their product comes.

Conservatives must not have anticipated the cheating, drunkenness, debauchery and sexual assaults that are now rampant among college campuses across the country. In the end, maybe this group of cognitive elites was saved by the fact that the students on those campuses had no weapons at hand. Coors then joined forces with the ultra-conservative heir of the Mellon fortune to fund the Analysis and Research Association (1971-1972) in Washington D.C., which became the one of the most influential right-wing think tanks in American politics. It then renamed itself The Heritage Foundation. Under the pretext of a benign non-profit agency, it spends most of its budget hiring like-minded thinkers to disseminate self-serving political messages that are designed to mold public attitudes and opinions. Changing America's very thinking has now gone commercial with no holds barred.

These well-funded, corporate-backed think tanks also joined forces with other elitist organizations like The Hudson Institute, The J. Howard Pew Foundation, The Olin Foundation, The Cato Institute, The Smith Richardson Foundation, The Coors Castle Rock Foundation, The Manhattan Foundation, The American Enterprise Foundation, and a host of others. (Brouwer, 2004) The resources poured into these elitist think tanks alone should indicate the seriousness of their intent. These wildly successful champions of privilege and plutocracy have infiltrated into every walk of life. Along with their conservative media, they have become the self-proclaimed experts on everything, and they don't appear to have the best interest of their inferiors in mind. A place for everyone is hardly a part of their agenda. These are the masterminds and the representatives of the affluent -the cognitive elite- who, as evidenced, lost touch with their deeper selves a long time ago. As the erudite Noam Chomsky has clearly shown, their primary concerns involve subjugating people with words, **weakening** governmental structures, oppression of the less powerful, class warfare and a permanent war economy.

Writing about politics since the 80's, Steve Brouwer confirmed that, "Occasionally conservative foundations have supported new *Social Darwinism* research such as Charles Murray's influential, *The Bell Curve* (lavishly funded by the Bradley Foundation and the Pioneer Foundation). In this way they were emulating the race research funded by the old Robber Barons and Skull and Bones crowd a century earlier, when they were infatuated with eugenics and the good breeding techniques required to reproduce the upper class." In his book, *Robbing Us Blind*, Brouwer goes on to state that the new wave of separatists tries to avoid the old racist claims to wealth and power, instead interfering more and more in the areas of politics and economics and their new form of stealthy and sordid, political and economic enslavement.

Some years after Brouwer's revealing publication, our politicians have done away with any tact and diplomacy, now openly instigating the angry racist behavior that creates the divisiveness they seek. Economic and political analyst, Robert Kuttner averred that the already popular idea of laissez-faire works well with the devil-may-care attitude of the powerful. Speaking about the desires of the privileged to breed people like themselves, Mark Twain noted: "Good breeding consists of concealing how much we think of ourselves, and how little we think of the other person."

As noted history professor, Michael B. Katz stated, "… Charles Murray's more sober and conventional *Losing Ground* provided conservatives with an authoritative argument against direct government spending to combat the undeniable growth of poverty." The unrelenting attack on social programs to help the needy is hidden behind the pretense of helping them. In 1981 a best-selling book by George Gilder, playing on the anti-intellectualism of the day, and using selected conservative writing, gave the administration even more fodder by which to justify cuts in social spending, while reducing taxes for the wealthy. Gilder's conservative tribute to wealth and inequality, *Wealth and Poverty,* was nothing less than the glorification of capitalism and its attendant greed.

Another of Murray's well-bred contemporaries, Robert Nozick, also contributed to the elitist onslaught with books that were declared, by one conservative reviewer, to be "the two most important books in political ethics since WWII." So as Murray and his cohorts legitimized social inequality and hailed wealth and privilege, they made clear their intentions to decimate groups of human beings, that they saw as undeserving of the prosperity that only they were entitled to, and moreover, these poor wretches were even deemed unworthy of basic sustenance.

As Katz continued to shine a light onto Murray's darkness we read: "Another assumption, not wholly consistent with the first, lurks just beneath the surface of Murray's argument. The first assumption justifies inequality with opportunity. The second assumes a harsh world of limited possibilities: "The tangible incentives that any society can realistically hold out to the poor youth of average abilities and average industriousness are mostly penalties, mostly disincentives." (*Losing Ground*) The author goes on to point out what we may have already gathered: Murray's greatest desire is to end all support so that all the indigent are allowed to do is to work hard and gain little. "Social policy must therefore emphasize the stick rather than the carrot." (*The Undeserving Poor,* 1989)

After outlining Murray's assertions concerning social welfare and social spending, denying that poverty is closely associated to crime and antisocial behavior, declaring that black unemployment increased because blacks voluntarily quit working, assuming that the increase in single female households was due to blacks who were disinterested in marriage, Murray opines that this and more were all due to social help programs. He mistakenly reasoned that these so-called incentives were the result of faulty, erroneous social policies of the mid-sixties, that we now know had just begun to lift people up. In a conclusive statement about Murray's dark logic, Katz remarks, "All these assertions, as one commentator after another has shown, are wrong."

Upon reviewing Murray's assessment of the sociopolitical situation in the mid-nineties, it is no wonder that in their greatest hour of need, the least among us were condemned to perpetual poverty and despair. It seems obvious to anyone who has the eyes to see, that this is the foundation upon which our house of cards now stands. Nothing could sum up ego inflation and the dark ideology of those who would be king as the words of Charles Murray himself: "Some people are better than others. They deserve more of society's rewards, of which money is only one small part." (*Losing Ground*)

There are a few other concepts germane to these discussions that we would like to talk about. Though it was circumvented by The Bell Curve, it is a term that has been distorted to the advantage of those who have been obsessed about proving others inferior. It was Herbert Spencer who first misused the term "survival of the fittest." His was a misguided notion derived from Darwin's theory of evolution. It was then misapplied to influence how people thought about social conditions and those who were seen as weak or unfit. The happy marriage of a government that is permissive toward big business, with the survival of those seen as more worthy and important, was called *Social Darwinism*. It also became the prevailing philosophy of the late 19th century. This widely accepted ideology survived in Europe and the United States until World War I. It provided the kind of thinking that legitimized the economic and political ambitions of colonial powers. Those indefatigable ambitions to rule the world and everyone in it have never changed.

Author of a definitive text on sociology, Ian Robertson, has effectively shown that the idea of Social Darwinism was essentially used to justify the dominance of whites over nonwhites, of the rich over the poor, and the powerful over the weak. Described as a unilinear evolutionary theory, it was proven to have been fatally flawed. Its first problem was that it described but did not provide viable social change. It was also said to have offered no account of how or why societies should even move towards this Western notion. Secondly, and most relevant, is that the theory was based on faulty data. (*Sociology*, 1987)

The arguments for Social Darwinism were confined to protecting the most affluent citizens and property owners and ensuring their safety; later, these ideas were also successfully rejected. It is also important to note the similarities in the thinking of Herrnstein and Murray, who used data and statistics to bolster their demands for economic and political changes. Their slightly more sophisticated methods were specifically designed to influence others to join them in their cause, and once again, we theorize that we are drawn to things that are more deeply a part of us than we care to admit, or may even realize.

Much like today, the earlier supporters of Social Darwinism refused to support public education. At that time, their thinking also left them with no concerns for things like the public mail system, sanitary regulations, or the pesky regulations of business or trade at all. The ruse of the day did not go by the names of free enterprise and privatization. The miserly attitudes of these upstanding dignitaries was especially noticeable when it came to public assistance to the needy. Spencerists claimed that competition was just a law of life, and there was no outside remedy for people in poverty other than self-help. These ideas would later influence the uncharitable policies of benign neglect in the 70's, on into 2020, where the new strategy is to pretend like poverty doesn't even exist, and it is never spoken of in a serious manner. And, as we've learned, avoidance and denial are powerful psychological defenses.

Advocates of Spencer and these stingy policies also declared that any interference to help the undesirables in their struggle just to exist, by the state or by any unwise philanthropy, would allow them to multiply, which could only result in a disastrous weakening of the species. It was in fact Spencer who coined the term "survival of the fittest." Darwin hadn't mentioned the human species in his classic volume *On the Origin of the Species* (Robertson, 1987). At this stage we can only imagine that their images of the struggling poor, breeding like vermin, were very troubling.

One can only speculate how a human being could reach a place in their lives that would allow them to watch others suffer needlessly while they lived in the lap of luxury. When we look at the possible reasons for a sclerosis of the human spirit, we can see that so many people judge their worth by material gain. They measure their worth by what they have and what they look like, thereby inevitably making them feel emptier and emptier inside, as they struggle to get their next fix. This doesn't demand our disdain, this calls for our pity. To have everything but yourself can be a very lonely and empty existence.

In the sixties, one of the most controversial studies on obedience to authority was conducted at Yale University by Professor Stanley Milgram. We bring up the study as an example of how much power intellectuals and other people in positions of power can have over others. And while the experiment may have been considered controversial at the time, its valuable findings are still being discussed today. It ended up successfully demonstrating just how willing some people are to harm others, based on their compliance to legitimate authority. It may also apply to those who might mistakenly believe that someone has that much power and authority.

The Milgram experiment began with one group of volunteers on one side of a wall administering electric shocks (that participants believed were from 15 volts to 450 volts) to a volunteer on the opposite wall, who was an accomplice of the experimenter. And although in a later debriefing, the volunteers were informed that no actual shock had been administered, this later presented some ethical issues for some.

As the experiment progressed the volunteers administering the shock would be pressured to continue increasing the intensity of the shock when the other participant gave the wrong answer to a question. Even though many of those rendering the shocks may have felt themselves to be moral and decent, the vast majority (at times troubled and hesitant) would go on to dole out up to 450 volts, in spite of the staged agonizing on the other side of the wall. Much like in other situations that can become dangerous, the volunteers in this study would later go on to rationalize that they were "just following orders."

So when we ask ourselves about man's inhumanity to man, and how people can hurt each other, we must keep in mind that the answers are never that easy. What we do know is that when people are unaware of their own darkness and inner turmoil, that they are more likely to project those negative energies onto others. This can involve people at both ends of the bell curve. There is one more disturbing concept that was not mentioned. The German word *schadenfreude* means pleasure that is derived from the misfortunes of others. People who enjoy watching the pain and suffering of other human beings embody the darkness of human nature. In leaving this segment, we turn to the words of a well-known American and Trappist monk, Thomas Merton.

"The great malady of the twentieth century, implicated in all our troubles and affecting us individually and socially, is the loss of soul."

Still intrigued by many components of the machine that produces suffering and inhumanity, we review the concept of *psychological archetypes*. The idea of *archetypes* was first used by Plato, Philo Judaeus and other early thinkers. The psychological feature of the word has been implemented more recently by thinkers like C.G. Jung, who made important and useful contributions to the way we see the human psyche and ourselves. Jung's valuable contributions to modern thought have tacitly influenced scholars and students in many areas like: cultural history, mythology, anthropology, theology, comparative religion and literary interpretation.

A basic definition of the term as used in psychology, is the characteristic and universal patterns that repeat themselves over and over in the psyches of human beings. These patterns are considered as pre-existing images in the collective psyche of the human race. Appearing ad infinitum, they have been shown to determine the basic ways in which we perceive and function as thinking and feeling beings.

Jung first discovered the existence of the psychological archetypes when as a psychiatrist, he studied mythology and symbolism and began using them in his empirical psychology and his clinical work. He discovered that the symbolic images that arise in people's dreams and fantasies often correspond exactly to images that have appeared in ancient art, myths and religions, from times and places from which the dreamer could not possibly have known. How many people in the world have not had experiences around the universal images of life, birth, death, anger, fear, joy, hate etc.? The implications of this discovery are extraordinary, if we could see past what we've been taught in an effort to appreciate a different way of understanding. At this point in our existential struggles, can we really afford not to give these ideas serious consideration? When speaking about power earlier, it may not have been clear that power itself is considered an archetype, as people are constantly trying to gain or maintain power over others everywhere. These patterns that we see time and time again are more often chalked up to just bad behavior, or maybe to human instinct. We would assert that some of the darkest behavior that we witness today in the world i.e. war, hate, violence etc. have at their core, archetypal origins. While many of these ideas might help us begin to understand this nefarious behavior, only we as individuals can change it. We also suggest that this can only happen when we make **significant** and **meaningful** changes within ourselves, and this is a task of monumental proportions. Mark Twain also observed that everyone talks about change, but nobody really changes.

We also propose that the variety of issues that we are discussing are connected and related. From politics to religion, and science to psychology, we are united by our common humanity. And as the great American Indians and other cultures have quietly admonished, we are all being summoned to the *great awakening*. The ideas that are rooted in the human psyche do not devalue or exclude science **or** religion, as hinted at by valued scientists like Einstein, Capra, Pauli and others.

Supporting our earlier notions on the need for a collaboration of science and religion (or spirituality), in a personal letter to one of his colleagues, the Nobel laureate Wolfgang Pauli wrote: "When he speaks of 'reality' the layman usually means something obvious and well known whereas it seems to me that precisely the most important and extremely difficult task of our time is to work on elaborating a new idea of reality. This is also what I mean when I always emphasize that science and religion *must* be related in some way." It is also important to note that these ideas are not necessarily in support of institutionalized or organized religion.

Closely associated with power and elitist thinking is a sense of superiority and the need to control, which fall under the umbrella of ego inflation, and are at the core of fascist ideology. This misuse of power is always a threat to freedom and equality everywhere and instead of it decreasing with our high IQ's, it has become more and more widespread.

In his most recent and informative book, *How Fascism Works* (2018), Yale professor Jason Stanley shares his valuable insight about a way of thinking that has spread carnage and destruction the world over. Dr. Stanley himself was a child of WWII refugees in Europe and is a renowned philosopher that has considerable knowledge about how propaganda works.

Earlier, we provided examples that were tactics used by those in positions of power to persuade others about "natural laws." This of course served the elitists thinkers of their day in getting what they wanted. They too saw the benefits of twisting and distorting language and faith to their advantage. As community leaders and figures of authority, they carefully crafted the language and speech that would shape the way in which people thought at the time, which also influenced their actions and behavior. Hiding behind the pretense of fairness and concern, early elitists also saw themselves as superior and entitled. Using various ploys and methods, and the gullibility of their subjects -much like today- they surreptitiously took control and were able to separate the wheat from the chaff. The chaff of course becoming their targeted scapegoats.

Borrowing only a few ideas from Stanley's work, we begin with the basic idea that fascist ideologues clearly understand the tendency of humans to organize society in a hierarchical fashion. Stanley also asserts that, "This principle of equality is a denial of natural law, which sets certain traditions, those of the most powerful over others. Their natural law allegedly places men over women, and members of the chosen nation of the fascist over other groupings." This is easily observable today, with the current leaders who praise white nationalism, while fomenting and targeting all Muslim people for the actions of a few extremists. In their zeal to unrealistically purge the world of radical extremists, they end up assisting in the recruitment of more, who see themselves as being under siege. And they conveniently overlook the extremists in their own midst (e.g. American Neo-Nazis and white extremists). Immigrants also become an easy, defenseless target. Dr. Stanley continues to explain how fascist rhetoric has repeatedly invoked nature for its own self-serving purposes. In 1861, the infamous *Cornerstone Speech*, delivered by the vice-president of the Confederacy illustrates the misuse of terms and the denigration of others, even back then. This rhetoric was used by the powerful in order to convince others of their superiority over those seen as less than: "Our government is founded upon exactly the opposite idea (of equality); its foundations are laid, its cornerstone rests, upon the great truth that the negro is not equal to the white man; that slavery and subordination to the superior race is his natural and normal condition." This pejorative speech has only become slightly more sophisticated in modern times, and Stanley remarks that it "… denounces the principle of liberty and equality enshrined in the U.S. Constitution as violations of the laws of nature."

This may also suggest that a significant number of naive or willfully ignorant people were willing to overlook their "do unto others" values to scapegoat a whole race of human beings. Having learned nothing from the past, thousands continue to be persecuted and slaughtered at the hands of those whose hate and angry projections have led us to a place where no amount of prayers or positive thinking may redeem us.

Professor Stanley's contribution is a painful reminder of just how quickly the rhetoric of failure can taint and distort our reality. Its negative effects on social policies, and a lack of concern for the most vulnerable members of our society can be witnessed in the news and on street-corners throughout this great nation.

Stanley's own clear understanding of democracy is exhibited when he stresses that "… the idea behind liberal democracy is that all of us are equally deserving of the basic goods of society." Of course others may have more skills and ambition, but it is the promise of opportunity and the hope of a brighter tomorrow that moves many people forward. In regards to fabricated hierarchical differences, Stanley points out that those differences are supported by no persuasive evidence and he asserts that, "Establishing hierarchies of worth is of course a means of obtaining and retaining power."

In a final statement regarding hierarchy, and coinciding with our observations on the pigeonholing in the Bell Curve, we read: "Those who strenuously argue for racial hierarchies of intelligence or the capacity for self-control, while denying any interest in illiberal, moral or political consequences, tend to be misguided."

While Dr. Stanley outlines a variety of methods used in fascist strategies, we will only mention the most obvious without going into detail: propaganda is a major technique, along with deceit, mendacity, fear-mongering, scapegoating, inciting violence, and the ever-effective method of creating a sense of loss in the general public. In America at least, most of these methods have a familiar ring. Convincing already-angry and frustrated people that they are being victimized and taken advantage of by people who look or act differently is precisely the modern day scapegoating method that promotes more anger, divisiveness, and eventually, violence and mayhem. Added to the arsenal of tyrants are the sordid strategies of pro-patriarchy, attacks on intellectuals and the media, the denigration of females and the feminine (misogyny), falsely charging others with the corruption they fail to see in themselves, and, offering simple solutions to complicated problems.

Denial and avoidance make it difficult to recognize the real miscreants in their very midst. As already noted, it is tragic but revealing, to realize that the ancient technique of *divide and conquer* is still such an effective weapon.

Directly related to our observations, and to the elitist mindset that would shred the fabric of our democratic principles, Dr. Stanley notes.

"It is classic fascist politics… to represent the actual defenders of liberal democracy as defending its ideals, only in the service of undermining them." In finishing out with Stanley's work it is important to re-emphasize that fascist principles become the most viable in times of economic hardship and when nations are in decline.

Levin Professor of History at Yale University, and awarded author Timothy Snyder states clearly, "To experience its destruction is to see a world for the first time. Inheritors of an order we did not build, we are now witness to a decline we did not foresee." Then, speaking to actually seeing ourselves as Americans one and all, and addressing the unending conflict and inequality, he declares that this would require "seeing all Americans as a citizenry rather than as groups in conflict." Heraclitus once declared that it was not things that bothered people, but rather, the way they viewed those things. Some groups are painted as problem people, rather than people with problems. Snyder's valuable and incisive theories around "the politics of eternity and the politics of inevitability" can be found in the riveting volume we are alluding to entitled, *The Road to Unfreedom* (2018). And, as he so ably predicts, "America will have both forms of equality, racial and economic, or it will have neither. If it has neither, eternity politics will prevail, racial oligarchy will emerge, and American democracy will come to a close."

In this most critical time in our history, and within this most exigent moment, comes the chance for a significant, meaningful change. If we are to move forward, then we must know ourselves well enough to know the truth. The ancient Chinese symbol for crisis speaks to the precarious place that we find ourselves in today. While on the one hand, it of course represents crisis, on the other hand it stands for opportunity. In the end, maybe what we are facing will determine whether our cognitive superiority will prevail, whether our souls will find redemption, and whether or not we will live up to the glorified title of *homo sapiens*.

Afterword

We hold firmly to the notion that the true measure of any person's worth cannot be calculated by IQ tests and standard deviation points. In regards to correlational studies, research can be tainted or skewed by a number of different factors to include: experimenter bias, the actual subjects chosen for a representative sample group, subject bias, the structure of interview questions and other problems. For example, one of the limits of correlational studies is that a consistent relationship between two factors is not always causal. In fact, sometimes a third factor could be involved. Consequently, a common mistake is made in the **interpretation** of these studies. People often conclude that because two factors are related, one causes the other and as mentioned, this is only true part of the time. (Crooks & Stein, 1988)

So it is generally accepted that it is dangerous to read too much into the findings of correlational studies. When a determined researcher sets out to prove or confirm what they already believe to be valid, then it isn't difficult to see how their testing, data, inferential statistics and interpretations can sometimes be directed by their own views and purposes. Cultural bias in IQ testing was not discussed in the volume we've reviewed. Snyder and Rothman have pointed out that it is "virtually impossible" to avoid "built-in biases" in designing and evaluating testing, that may favor some test subjects, while placing others at a disadvantage (ibid., 1988). So, more often, only different and more objective research and testing on the same topic can and may reduce findings down to a more accurate account.

Numerous studies have shown that while psychologists do not dispute the fact that, on average, blacks score lower on IQ tests than whites, they've also theorized that improving educational and socioeconomic conditions has a significant impact on IQ scores as well. And, as a researcher in that same text asserts, "IQ differences between the races are beginning to shrink" (Jones, 1984). While this sounds promising, at the same time, it may also be disturbing to those who see it as somehow unacceptable, because it threatens those who are fearful and insecure. As suggested earlier in our text, some people will use any means necessary to hold on to what they value most and what they most identify with -money, power, status and things.

Even a staunch supporter of the idea of the heritability of intelligence, Arthur Jensen (a controversial educational psychologist), after investigating the IQ scores of white and black children in Georgia in 1977, concluded that the "cumulative deficit" found only among blacks could not be accounted for by genetic factors. To the contrary, his investigation provided clear evidence that impoverished educational and economic environments severely curtail the opportunities for intellectual growth (Crooks & Stein, 1988).

Considering the current assault on education and the impoverished, perhaps it was even prescient for the renowned Michael Harrington to have said, "When we join in solidarity and not in noblesse oblige, with the poor, we will rediscover our own best selves… we will regain the vision of America."

Outside ourselves we observe an ocean of darkness and problems, but all the while, the squalls are being generated by us. The fear, anger, greed and hatred that we see out there on a macro-level are merely a reflection of what is going on inside of us on a micro-level. It has been our contention all along, that science alone will not pull us back from the precipice. While we can't turn our back on science, *scientism* is a belief that the methods of the physical sciences are applicable or justifiable in all fields of inquiry. And yet, if you believe such things exist, these methods will never be able to measure or define *soul* and *spirit*. At this point, science can only theorize and postulate, "… as the fallacy of believing that the method of science must be used on all forms of experience and, given time, will settle every issue" (Jacques Barzun).

Esteemed evolutionary biologist, Richard Lewontin, while commenting on unquestioned materialistic explanations remarked that, "One restricts one's questions to the domain where materialism is unchallenged." We know that some scientific research has been compromised by big money interests and that even the professional scientific reports in reputable journals are coming into question. As mentioned, the long held belief in the Cartesian/Newtonian scientific view is quickly becoming an outdated paradigm. While there are many ideas and discoveries within that model that will always maintain their significance, time waits for no one. On the other hand, it is also advisable to avoid religiosity and psychologism, even though everything that makes us intelligent, sentient beings emanates from the psyche. The noted scientific philosopher, Karl Popper proclaimed that "Science can never produce knowledge that is certain, or even probable." These ideas may leave thinking people who yearn for definitive answers in the lurch, but it should give us all reason to ponder why we so desperately search for the answers to everything outside ourselves, and yet, see little or no value in what lies within us.

Scientific reductionism and causality are valuable theories that do not apply when attempting to explain the structure and behavior of the unconscious. At this time, this part of the psychological realm is a mysterious area in which some normally useful scientific methods are limited and relatively ineffective. Physicist P.W. Bridgman stated that "… the structure of nature may eventually be such that our processes of thought do not correspond to it sufficiently to permit us to think about it at all… The world fades out and eludes us… We have reached the limit of the great pioneers of science, the vision, namely, that we live in a sympathetic world in that it is comprehensible by our minds."

Given these challenging assertions, and the existential dilemma of a split and divided world, we are now being summoned to see things in a way that is not so black and white after all. It seems that the opposites we spoke of earlier need to be, not only understood, but even reconciled. In Hegelian theory, nature itself, human history and culture were the expressions of a dialectical process. Basically, the first stage of the process is the initial issue, subject or situation and is called the *thesis*. The second phase is then referred to as the *antithesis*, which is a time when things fall apart, a phase of conflict or duality. The third and final stage then is the *synthesis*, in which things are rejoined, reunited. The only difficulty in reaching this final phase, is the question of whether we find ourselves and come together, or we are consumed by the ego inflation that destroys. Any real advancement is accomplished both internally **and** externally. For those who would identify with a god-like power, my personal observation is that there is no such thing as perfection, and that they are deities who defecate.

To be inclusive of others may also mean that we possess a deeper understanding of the "other" that lies within. The projections of our darker nature onto those who do not meet our myopic demands and expectations is clearly indicative of a fragmented personality and a limited existence. So important it is to know yourself that above the entrance-way to the temple of Delphi (Apollo's temple) are the words, "Know Thyself" inscribed in stone, so that we are constantly reminded of just how important this simple principle really is. Simple only in principle, it is obviously difficult to achieve. Besides, how can we find ourselves, if we don't see ourselves.

In the well-received volume, The Bell Curve, the authors and the book's supporters made a great effort, using the abundance of resources at their disposal, to magnify the differences and imperfections of others. It is our understanding that there are many other people who would have preferred some resources spent on outlining what we have in common. Having already mentioned the uproar and the projections from all sides, we would suggest here that we may all have a little work to do. This does not minimize its damaging effects that still resonate today.

We may never be free of war, conflict and anger, as they are considered as the deeply ingrained, archetypal patterns that must be addressed by each of us on a deeper level. We can and must however make an honest attempt to mitigate the behavior that is a result of the emergence of that unconscious content. Also, as mentioned, the real battle wages on **within**.

Returning to our psychological lens, we go directly to the Indo-Germanic root *angh*, from where we derive the word *anger*, which basically means "to constrict." What is evident is that virtually all modern socialization processes tend to restrict natural human impulses, therefore it is usually unacceptable to express anger, particularly in public. Since this is a natural impulse that comes over most of us at times, some of that unexpressed anger doesn't go away. Consequently, a build-up of anger is to be expected. Most of us know that the downside here is that anger can only be suppressed for so long, and then it may be expressed in ways that are damaging and hurtful.

This has been likened to filling a bag with crap, and continuing to fill it until it can hold no more. Of course, when it reaches its full capacity the bag has a tendency to explode and the crap goes everywhere. We are not always as in control as we would like to think. And when these issues are deeply entrenched in an individual then outer remedies like anger management have a very limited effect. Moreover, if this natural impulse is considered a weakness or a moral failure (i.e. sinful) then it is apparent that the "wrongdoer" can experience a troubling inner conflict, which can in itself lead to other erratic or troubling behavior.

Suffice it to say that we are still responsible for the behavior that occurs when this unwanted energy surfaces. And much like other unconscious content, if it is not addressed effectively it is acted out or it is turned inward, where it can cause mental or physical illness. An Analytical psychologist might suggest that the ideal situation, inasmuch as there is one, is to develop some degree of relatedness to our own inner images and energies -to know ourselves.

Another piece of the puzzle can be found in our primary experiences with authority, which are more often derived from our primary caregivers. While many of the interactions we have with our parents may be healthy and positive, sometimes they are not. Adults can later find themselves unwittingly checking in with the authority figures of the past, which can also create inner conflict and be confusing at times. Well-meaning teachers, religious figures and other adults can inadvertently create more harm than good in their efforts to demand obedience and uniformity from us.

In reality, the homogeneous society desired by the authors in our review would essentially mean a society of de-individualized drones who all acted and looked alike. This might be desirable to the despots who need to have dominance and control over others, but it also means a world filled with submissive individuals who lack a distinct and independent personality.

The natural feeling that occurs when one is excluded from a group is shame or guilt. Shaming, cajoling and ostracizing, along with other methods of persuasion can have a powerful effect when trying to convince others to comply to our way of thinking. And there are many people who seek power, from our homes to our government, who are ever so willing to exert their power over others and take control. When people can begin to acknowledge their own ability to make healthy decisions and take control of their own lives, then their authenticity begins.

Recognizing one's inner dependency on outer authority, often projected onto the state, the church, the boss or other "experts" and authority figures, we begin our journey of becoming free-thinking, independent human beings. Without this, we can become another member of the herd, vulnerable and susceptible to those who seem to have all the knowledge and control. Breaking away from mass man mentality may have its cost, but losing our integrity and who we are is a far higher price to pay.

Communities, having originated with groups, have a tendency to exert powerful deterrents over members to operate within the laws, norms and mores of the group. Manipulating words and information, instilling fear and playing on people's emotions go a long way in keeping people in lock step so they will continue to do our bidding. As in ancient times, losing the acceptance and approval of others was considered as one of the worst punishments that could be visited upon a person.

The concept of individualism played into the industrial and post-industrial society as a primary feature that ends up weakening the cohesiveness of communities. When individual desires become more important than traditional obligations and our communities, then a self-serving "What's in it for me" attitude is the consequence. The divisiveness we see in the world is a reflection of the disunity we find in ourselves.

Much like parental rejection and loss of approval, the loss of social acceptance is so powerful that people will shelve their own feelings and their own interests, going to great lengths to conform and do what others are doing, or what others want them to do. This creates a huge opening for opportunists, manipulators and other charismatic charlatans. It can also create a sense of confusion and a loss of self in the individual. Fortunes are made by capitalizing on those who have not accepted themselves for who they are. Caught up in the glitter and the glamour, we satisfy our hunger with materialism and toxic consumerism, but the next big thing only leaves us starving for more. Perhaps this is what is meant by selling one's soul.

Final Thoughts

We simply cannot solve the problems of today with the thinking of yesterday. We can however use the lessons and lore of the past to guide us to a better future. And though there is something to be said for tradition, a fair and equal society, where we live in harmony will not be obtained by intelligence testing and drowning ourselves with data and statistics. The past patterns of proving others to be less than we are or just "accepting the fact that people are unequal" only confirms how spiritually bankrupt and emotionally impoverished some of us have become. When we realize that in harming and oppressing others that we only hurt ourselves, then this is the beginning of wisdom. Along with the understanding that mutual cooperation is far more effective (and cohesive) than callous competition, as a way of seeing the world, just might save it.

We are constantly being seduced by the sirens of popular culture. And we can only wonder how much intelligence is found in the obsessive and popularized belief in endless growth and progress on a finite planet with limited and dwindling resources. Possibly what we lack in this country is not so much intelligence, but humility.

Insecurity, fear and self-doubt often serve as the fuel for the darkness that we project onto others. From a geocentric world view to a heliocentric perspective, the uncertainty about our world and about ourselves came into plain view. For it was at this time that we were no longer the center of the universe. It also brought the notion of anthropocentrism into question, and contributes to the existential crisis that we are now facing. It most certainly created a sense of alienation.

From Melville to Yeats, and from biblical lore to Goethe, the motif of alienation carries strong implications for all our lives. Stories, myths and poetry give expression to the mythological (i.e. archetypal) roots of the psyche –that *is* their attraction, their pull.

This theme of alienation holds particular relevance for us due to the fact that, except for the indigenous natives in this country, Americans are immigrants or descendants of immigrants who were uprooted from their mother countries and transplanted onto foreign soil –essentially, we are all aliens. And while Americans have always believed that the future (along with this country) was theirs, the lack of a past that is rooted in this land creates the ongoing feelings of cultural inferiority.

And this is compensated for by technological arrogance, toxic materialism, and projecting our fears and insecurities onto those seen as different and inferior. In the psychological realm, this is compounded by the *self-alienation* that is rampant in our society, whereby we are separated from each other, separated from nature, and separated from our own nature.

The basis of modern epistemology is essentially twofold: *rationalism* -secular humanism (the subjective mind), and *empiricism* -scientific materialism (the objective world) …what is and what ought to be? This intellectual journey seems to have led us from the sacred to the secular where the human mind was perceived as separate from, and superior to, nature. And yet, we are just as much a part of nature as it is a part of us. As the learned Richard Tarnas concluded: "Scientific materialism and scientific reductionism have reduced all of mankind itself." (*The Passion of the Western Mind*, 1991)

The epistemological uncertainty of the past is also the existential challenge of the present. Our unchallenged and unexplored values and beliefs have given us few sound answers and little respite in our quest for balance and harmony. Looking about us, it also seems as though, even fewer people have found happiness. And as past wisdom would indicate: "It seems to me a case of negligence if, after becoming firm in our faith, we do not strive to understand **what** we believe." St. Anselm (italics mine) This applies to our other beliefs as well.

Long ago in Persia, following a revelation from Ahura Mazda, Zoroastrianism began and it created a marked distinction between light and darkness, and consequently good from evil. As mentioned, religions borrowed from each other along the way and eventually this created a simplistic polarization between good and evil, a distinction that can no longer sustain us. Some would maintain a moral certitude leaning towards absolutism, however this one-sidedness has the tendency to switch to its opposite, and the evidence of this can be seen everywhere.

And while good and evil are real phenomena, there also appears to be at least a modicum of one or the other in the best and the worst among us. When certain images and their accompanying emotions are triggered in people, we can witness behavior that ranges from angelic to demonic, and sometimes this happens very quickly. Very simply put, there are not actually two separate categories of human beings -good and bad- we each have the capacity for both. Perhaps it is time for all of us to join in the cosmic dance together. And because it bears repeating, we have no more time for us and them thinking -it is time for **we**.

Bibliography

Brouwer, Steve. *Robbing Us Blind.* Monroe, ME: Common Courage Press, 2004

Crooks & Stein. *Psychology.* New York: Holt, Rinehart and Winston, Inc., 1988

Harrington, Michael. *The New American Poverty*. New York: Penguin Books, 1985

Herrnstein, Richard J. and Murray, Charles. *The Bell Curve*. New York: Free Press Paperbacks, 1994

Katz, Michael B. *The Undeserving Poor*. New York: Pantheon Books, 1989

Robertson, Ian. *Sociology*. New York: Worth Publishers Inc., 1987

Schwartz, Jeffrey M. *The Mind and the Brain*. New York: HarperCollins Publishers Inc., 2002

Stanley, Jason. *How Fascism Works*. New York: Random House, 2018

Author's Note: Every reasonable effort has been made to contact the copyright holders of all material reproduced in this book.